Praise for *Christianity in Blue*

"In *Christianity in Blue*, Kaden provides us with a rich and warm account of how progressive Christians read the Bible, seek to follow Jesus, and devote themselves to love above all in a beautiful yet hurting world."

—Matthew Thiessen, McMaster University

"Many people wonder whether there is a role for religion in today's world and, if there is, whether contemporary religion is only for the dogmatic or narrow-minded. I've sometimes wondered this myself. For those who wonder, Christians and non-Christians alike, this is *the* book to read. Kaden is that most unusual combination of a profound scholar who is also a dynamic church pastor. The book shows not only that religion is relevant in the world today but also that in a world of uncertainty that sometimes seems to spiral into chaos, religion can help people find meaning, purpose, and tranquility in life. Kaden presents a modern, progressive Christian view of the world that has been so elusive and often hidden in the public arena of Christianity today. This is one of the best books I've read in a long time. My life has been greatly enriched by it, as will any reader's!"

—Robert J. Sternberg, Cornell University and the University of Heidelberg, Germany

"A slender yet sweeping blueprint for how to read the Bible and live in community for those who want to embody the compassionate heart of the gospel. As a New Testament scholar and serving pastor, Kaden experiences Scripture as the foundational *starting point* for the Christian life, not an ideological dead end. *Christianity in Blue* is a timely antidote for those disheartened by evangelical Christianity's current glorification of judgment over love."

—Catherine E. Taylor, pastor of Presbyterian Church (USA)

"*Christianity in Blue* is for anyone who is troubled by the constrictive teachings, the conditional welcome, and the divide-and-conquer politics of many American churches today. Kaden's book is written in layperson's English (not in theologese). It should be required reading for all pastors, congregants, ex-churchgoers, and former Christians. If I had my way, I would stock it in every bookstore and in every church pew across America. It is that incisive. It is that important."

—Christopher Xenakis, pastor of Groton
Community Church, Groton, New York

"This book is a must read for anyone interested in a relevant and pragmatic understanding of progressive Christianity. Clergy, students, skeptics, scholars, and folks in the pews will find Kaden's perspective thoroughly informative and deeply illuminating. Filled with references from Kierkegaard to the Cure, it is both immensely scholarly as well as completely accessible."

—Richard Rose, pastor of First Baptist
Church, Painted Post, New York

CHRISTIANITY IN BLUE

CHRISTIANITY IN BLUE

HOW THE BIBLE, HISTORY, PHILOSOPHY, AND THEOLOGY SHAPE PROGRESSIVE IDENTITY

DAVID A. KADEN

FORTRESS PRESS

Minneapolis

CONTENTS

ACKNOWLEDGMENTS

This book has been percolating for years. I started scratching out notes and typing drafts more than fifteen years ago in my Harvard Divinity School days just as I began emerging from the confines of evangelicalism. Life encroaches, however. Plans change or are altered. Children arrive on the scene and are wonderfully disruptive. Completing a PhD is all-consuming. Serving churches as a minister is nearly all-consuming. New academic and pastoral writing projects press in from all sides. In short, this book was set on the back burner but never completely forgotten. I suppose I just wasn't ready to focus on it until recently.

Naturally, with so much lived experience between handwritten notes and the final manuscript, there are more people who helped write this book than can be named here, but a few people deserve special recognition. My ThM thesis advisor at Harvard, Elisabeth Schüssler Fiorenza, first gave me a progressive Christian paradigm to think with—interpreting the Bible and Christian tradition in ways that uplift instead of degrade and damage. I cite her extensively in this book. My PhD thesis advisor at the University of Toronto, John Kloppenborg, taught me how to think, study, and write as a scholar. My ministry mentor Catherine Taylor taught me how to take head knowledge and make it practical; she showed me how to be a pastor. The four years I worked with her were life changing for me. My close friend Rich Rose has taught me the power of compassion in ministry—the power of acceptance, mercy, grace, and love—the very foundation of progressive Christianity.

Many of the members and friends of First Congregational Church of Ithaca were in the writing room with me as this book took shape. I imagined hearing their questions, comments, suggestions, and even criticisms. This book is for them and for all who call themselves "progressive Christians."

I thank the editors of Fortress Press. They are professional, thorough, and also kind. They are a reminder that while few books in this world are great, no book is good or even good enough without good editors.

Finally, I thank my family. I am not the only writer in the Kaden clan, so I cherish the support of my parents and siblings as well as my partner and children. I tried very hard to write early in the morning or late at night to keep my kids from seeing me hunched over a computer keyboard during waking hours, especially as deadlines approached. I still reserved as much time as possible for Xbox with my son, movie watching with my daughter, and eating out with my wife. The finer things in life.

David A. Kaden, Lent 2021

1

WHAT IS *PROGRESSIVE* IN PROGRESSIVE CHRISTIANITY?

For centuries, Christianity has been presented as a system of beliefs. That system of beliefs has supported a wide range of unintended consequences, from colonialism to environmental destruction, subordination of women to stigmatization of LGBT people, anti-Semitism to Islamophobia, clergy pedophilia to white privilege. What would it mean for Christians to rediscover their faith not as a problematic system of beliefs, but as a just and generous way of life, rooted in contemplation and expressed in compassion, that makes amends for its mistakes and is dedicated to beloved community for all? Could Christians migrate from defining their faith as a system of beliefs to expressing it as a loving way of life?

—Brian McLaren, *The Great Spiritual Migration*

A religious community that believes itself to be in possession of "the Truth" is a community equipped with the most lethal weapon of any warfare: the sense of its own superiority and mandate to mastery.

—Douglas John Hall, *The Cross in Our Context*

"You're socially liberal *and* a theologian? How do you reconcile what the Bible says with how you see the world?" My cousin texted this question to me because she wanted clarity. In her mind, and in the minds of many, "liberal" and "what the Bible says" are at odds. For her and many others, "what the Bible says" are the four words guaranteed to shut down all critical thinking. They signal that God is an abusive and militaristic king-in-the-sky, that LGBTQ+ people are an abomination, that climate change is not a concern, that doubt is sinful, that abortion is murder, and that the pages of the Bible are filled with judgmentalism and a host of arcane moral rules. These words suggest that the only point of being a Christian is to enjoy postmortem bliss with angels and harps in heaven, that evolution is wrong, that Christians must be political conservatives, and that tax cuts for the rich are fine because Jesus once said the poor will always be with us. The list goes on and on.

But what if "what the Bible says" is open-ended? What if we viewed the Bible and our Christian tradition as conversation *starters* instead of as the final words on any topic? What if *we* decide within a community of fellow faith journeyers what our sacred text and sacred tradition can mean today? What if meaning is not something etched into the stones of the theological past but something living, changing, and always needing to be reforged for new times? What if we treated the Bible and Christian tradition as invitations to question, wonder, think critically, and then act with faith-driven purpose in celebration of our common humanity to change our world for the better?[1] My hope is that in reading this book, you will get excited about

---

1. I realize that in asking such questions, I am, as my scholar of religion colleagues would say, staking out an "emic," or insider, position as opposed to an "etic," or outsider, one. I have migrated between the two in my published work. See my first book, *Matthew, Paul, and the Anthropology of Law*

progressive Christianity, its vision for the world, its compassion for every human being and for all of creation, and its ancient roots in Christian tradition—what poet Christian Wiman calls "this strange, ancient thing."[2] I also hope you will gain a greater appreciation for the Bible, the sacred Christian text. More than just appreciating it, I hope you will feel liberated to doubt it, question it, interrogate it, and learn to read it in new ways.

I realize that in promoting a *progressive* Christianity, I am swimming against the current of recent writing that has criticized progressive Christianity from multiple directions. Conservatives have asserted that progressive Christianity is a kind of Christianity-lite, which avoids all talk of personal sin and champions superficial love. More radical critics charge that progressive Christianity clings too closely to ancient forms of theology without taking seriously enough the earthshaking significance of writers like Friedrich Nietzsche, Karl Marx, and Sigmund Freud. I also realize that using a category like "progressive Christianity" can be problematic for many reasons. I will address these criticisms and problems in due course, but I remain convinced that there are good reasons to be a progressive follower of Jesus Christ in the twenty-first century—reasons that are rooted and anchored in tradition and sound exegesis of the Bible, that are philosophically sophisticated, politically engaged, and personally and socially liberating.

I once believed that "what the Bible says" was the final word on pretty much every topic from ethics to politics to theology because I believed the Bible was inerrant (without error). The Bible for me was a conversation *closer*. Ironically, my views

---

Wissenschaftliche Untersuchungen zum Neuen Testament, no. 2 (Tübingen: Mohr Siebeck, 2016), for an example of etic writing.

2. Christian Wiman, *My Bright Abyss: Meditation of a Modern Believer* (New York: Farrar, Straus & Giroux, 2013), 91.

changed dramatically at an evangelical seminary where the Bible was revered as inerrant. While researching the doctrine of inspiration (the view that the Bible is inspired by God and thus error-free), I was surprised to discover how widespread the disagreement was among twentieth-century evangelical theologians over the meaning of the word *inerrant*. I struggled to find even two evangelical theologians who shared identical views on the topic. Some considered the Bible inerrant in its presentation of history, science, ethics, and theology. Others judged it inerrant only in its ethics and theology, since evolution has made a literal interpretation of the Bible's creation stories impossible, and plenty of discrepancies exist in the Bible's presentation of history. Still others argued that the Bible is inerrant with respect to its *intent*, even if its presentation of details is jumbled, while some insisted it was inerrant with respect to its *ideas* if not its exact words. I soon discovered that the word *inerrant* was an empty signifier, an identity marker without a stable meaning. As long as one says they believe the Bible is inerrant (in whatever way they choose to define the word), they can be in the evangelical club.[3]

But I came to believe that if evangelical Christianity was grounded in the belief that the Bible is God's inerrant word and the professional evangelical theologians couldn't agree on the meaning of the term, then I could no longer be an evangelical. If the central evangelical doctrine of inerrancy was emptied of

---

3. See, for example, R. C. Spoul, "The Chicago Statement on Biblical Inerrancy," in *Explaining Inerrancy* (Orlando: Ligonier Ministries, 1996), 59–74. The Chicago Statement contains nineteen articles that defend biblical inerrancy. It defines *inerrancy* as "the quality of being free from all falsehood or mistake and so safeguards the truth that Holy Scripture is entirely true and trustworthy in all its assertions." Spoul, 71. The two operative phrases are "free from all falsehood" and "trustworthy in all its assertions," both of which leave room for wide-ranging and even contradictory interpretations.

meaning, then the entire evangelical edifice was, for me, a house of cards. I graduated from an evangelical seminary with the highest honors but no longer self-identified as an evangelical.

I went on to Harvard Divinity School (a decision that two of my former professors tried to talk me out of), served churches as a minister, and eventually completed a PhD in the academic study of religion at the University of Toronto's Department for the Study of Religion. In these quite different academic settings, I learned to think critically as a scholar and to deal in a world of evidence-based reasoning, skepticism, uncertainty, the careful application of a method, and clear argumentation. In both schools, I met thoughtful Christians who were critical, open about their doubts and questions, and yet committed to being followers of Christ within the church. One of my advisors at Harvard was an ordained minister in the Swiss Reformed Church and would speak eloquently about his personal faith. Another was a leading feminist theologian and a faithful Catholic. My gospels professor was ordained in the Lutheran Church and a committed Christian who preached regularly in his home church near Boston. One of my professors at U of T had an encyclopedic knowledge of modern Christian theology and remains a dedicated Anglican who leads prayers in his home cathedral. As both critical scholars and serious Christians, they taught me to think for myself and to evolve both as an academic and as a Christian.

In my evangelical seminary days, I was taught that homosexuality was an abomination and that doubt in matters of faith was a sin. But at Harvard and Toronto, I met students who were both committed Christians and openly gay, pursuing ordination in their home denominations. I also met students and faculty who took solace in liberal thinkers such as Paul Tillich, a theologian notable for being honest about doubt and serious about faith. Meeting these "liberal" Christians, listening to their stories, hearing about their personal testimonies, and reading their books and articles were completely eye-opening. These people became human beings to me, *Christian* human beings with flesh-and-blood stories. They were not the heretics that I had been warned about. They were not objects to be despised and sneered at. They were people. Followers of Christ who digested Scripture, albeit critically; prayed fervently; attended church regularly; and changed my life.

Like Ati, the protagonist in Boualem Sansal's novel *2084* whose life was transformed when he realized that there was a whole other world beyond the borders of his narrow, conservative religious one, I had an experience of irrevocable liberation. "A bird that leaves its cage, even just for a single flap of its wings," Sansal writes, "cannot return."[4]

I went on to teach in colleges and universities in Canada and the United States but felt a pull back to the church. I am now a minister in the United Church of Christ (UCC)—one of America's most progressive Christian denominations. I am a committed progressive Christian and an academic who has fled the cage of conservatism. I study the Bible with the critical eye of a scholar and with the openness of a believer, and I serve a church in a college town.

I am a UCC minister in Ithaca, New York. Ithaca is named after the kingdom of Odysseus, the Greek hero of the Homeric epic, and is home to Cornell University and Ithaca College. Ithaca is also a haven of natural beauty—gorges, waterfalls, Cayuga Lake, sweeping landscapes—each the result of sliding glaciers from the last ice age some ten thousand years ago.

---

4. Boualem Sansal, *2084: The End of the World*, trans. Alison Anderson (New York: Europa Editions, 2017), 38.

"Ithaca is gorges" is a common slogan here. As a college town isolated by hills, gorges, and lots of water (or, as some snidely call it, "ten square miles surrounded by reality"), Ithaca is a teeming hive of wineries, microbrew pubs, sports bars, theaters, local mom-and-pop stores, hemp stores, coffee shops, farmers' markets, tattoo parlors, and two of the groups most hostile to organized religion: millennials and ex-hippie baby boomers. I sometimes joke with my clergy friends that if a church can thrive here in Ithaca, it can thrive anywhere. Ithaca is a town where there is a good chance the local barista has a PhD, a geologist lives next door to you, and people will hang rainbow flags instead of American flags on their front porches (or sometimes hang both flags next to each other). But it is also a town of straitlaced lawyers and business types, professors, students, and small-business owners. Ithaca is eclectic.

My church is as eclectic as Ithaca itself. Our membership includes Cornell and Ithaca College professors and students, university and college administrators, school teachers, shop managers, lawyers, retirees, stay-at-home dads and moms, doctors, bankers, employees of nonprofits, librarians, museum curators, social workers, quilters, potters, scientists, vegans, Shakespeare scholars, real estate agents, art historians, economists, musicians and singers, novelists, painters, LGBTQ+ advocates, peace and justice activists, ex-clergy, retired clergy, recovering evangelicals, recovering Catholics, practicing Catholics, doubters, atheists, agnostics, practicing Jews, and even Buddhists. Our worship is traditional, as are our prayers and liturgies, but our theology is not. Our Christian tradition, like our Bible, is a conversation *starter* and not the final word on any topic. As a progressive Christian church, we proudly wave a rainbow flag on our front lawn, talk about God as a "She" or "Mother," critically read passages in the Bible against each other, and openly acknowledge our doubts and questions. We take seriously the fact that each one of us is on our own spiritual journey—a journey that will twist and turn over sometimes rocky, craggy terrain and is as unpredictable as life itself.

In spite of this up-and-down reality of the faith journey, one thing we all share in common in our church—and I include myself in this "we all" because I too have doubts and questions and struggle at times with skepticism and uncertainty on *my* journey of faith—is that we value our Christian heritage, our sense of rootedness in a deep, rich tradition. We sing old hymns, we regularly recite the ancient Lord's Prayer, and we appreciate the homiletic challenge of the sermon that updates our Christian tradition for today. In the spirit of the earliest Christians, we share dish-to-pass meals and care for those in need. In the spirit of the Hebrew prophets, we work for justice in our town and world. In the spirit of Jesus, we try to treat everyone we meet as a beloved child of God. In the spirit of people of faith all over the world, we believe there is more to life than the bland, bourgeois materialism that forces us to grind out a daily existence to pay bills and save for retirement while running endless errands and carting our kids off to their ever-growing number of activities. And with our forebears in the Christian faith, we share a common love for a two-thousand-year-old text that we call "Scripture," from which we draw inspiration to guide our journeys of faith. We strive to be examples of the Christian left in the twenty-first century: a thriving, vibrant, active and activist, hopeful, faithful, loving, peacemaking, justice-oriented, and welcoming mainline Christian church.

As progressive Christians, we believe that a robust, thought-provoking faith, like a good piece of art, can enhance life and make it savory. A thoughtful, robust faith can slow us down and spark in us a sense of awe at the natural world. Philosopher

Slavoj Žižek claims that Christianity leads to a sturdy materialism—an appreciation of the here and now—in part because the central story of Christianity is one of God taking on flesh to become like us.[5] Or as writer Peter Rollins starkly notes, "Christianity can be described as a theological materialism: It is that which transforms our material existence. If our faith does not throw us into the arms of the world, if it does not lead to our experience of responsibility, love, celebration, and our commitment to transformation, then, whatever we call it, we have nothing but an empty shell."[6]

The famous astronomer Carl Sagan (himself a citizen of Ithaca) expressed well his appreciation of the natural world when he admitted that he felt the "religious sensibility, the sense of awe" when "look[ing] up on a clear night,"[7] overwhelmed by what Protestant Reformer John Calvin once called a "dazzling theater."[8] In the UCC, we have a slogan:

Be the church.

Protect the environment.

Care for the poor.

Forgive often.

Reject racism.

Fight for the powerless.

Share earthly and spiritual resources.

---

5. Slavoj Žižek, *The Puppet and the Dwarf: The Perverse Core of Christianity* (Cambridge, MA: MIT Press, 2003), 6, 13.

6. Peter Rollins, *Insurrection: To Believe Is Human, to Doubt, Divine* (New York: Howard Books, 2011), 156.

7. Carl Sagan, *The Varieties of Scientific Experience: A Personal View of the Search for God* (New York: Penguin, 2006), 2.

8. John Calvin, *Institutes of the Christian Religion*, ed. John T. McNeill, trans. Ford Lewis Battles, 2 vols., Library of Christian Classics 20 (Louisville, KY: Westminster John Knox, 1960) I.v.8, 61.

Embrace diversity.

Love God.

Enjoy this life.

The emphasis of progressive Christianity is on *this* life and on changing *this* world for the benefit of people *now*. We believe this world is God's world—something to be enjoyed, relished, celebrated, and improved in our communities, families, and neighborhoods. We try to live fully *in* God, the source of life, soaking up life's moments and embracing them with the wonder of a child.

A robust and progressive Christian faith makes us more empathetic and more compassionate people. We progressive Christians cling closely to Christ, who is, according to our tradition, what God is like in flesh. Notwithstanding the various inconsistencies in the stories about Jesus Christ in the New Testament gospels, one constant theme that emerges even on a cursory reading of these four accounts is a picture of Jesus as a deeply compassionate person who embraced outsiders. When perusing the gospels, it would be difficult to remain unmoved after encountering the openheartedness of the Good Samaritan in the parable Jesus once told about him, or after sitting with Jesus and the woman at the well as he embraced her in spite of her otherness, or after reading about Jesus crossing all sorts of social barriers to heal a leper with a touch or to forgive the sins of a prostitute as she wept near his feet. Bishop John Shelby Spong once wrote of "the boundary-breaking love that we meet in the life of Jesus." Spong continues,

> When a human being [i.e., Jesus] appears in history with
> a greater ability to love than we have ever knowingly wit-
> nessed before, when this life calls us into a new human unity

> and refuses to be bound by the rules that rise out of our incompleteness and our fear, then we inevitably look at that life with awe. . . . Love is a presence and power that calls us out of tribal fears for it embraces Jew and Gentile, and out of prejudice-spawning fears for it embraces whoever is our Samaritan. Love has no chosen people, for that implies that some are unchosen. Love bears no malice, seeks no revenge, guards no doorway.[9]

After reading about this boundary-breaking love of Jesus, U2 singer Bono said, "If only we could be a bit more like [Jesus], the world would be transformed."[10]

It is precisely because we strive to follow the example of Jesus—embracing outsiders, loving neighbors and enemies, and working toward wholeness, justice, and peace—that we progressive Christians are deeply moved by what our tradition calls sin and evil in the world. We grieve at tragedy, suffering, violence, and victimization. We believe that *God* grieves at these evils, which is why we work with God's spirit to change both ourselves and our world. We are driven by the songs of the Hebrew prophets, who dreamed of a day when swords would be beaten into plowshares, spears would be refashioned into pruning hooks, the world's wolves and lambs would dwell together in peace, and justice would roll down like water. This vision, this dream—*God's Dream*, as Archbishop Desmond Tutu calls it—imagines a day when warring and violence, injustice and oppression will end and when the implements (and

---

9. John Shelby Spong, *A New Christianity for a New World: Why Traditional Faith Is Dying and How a New Faith Is Being Born* (San Francisco: HarperSanFrancisco, 2001), 139–40.

10. Frank Viola, "Bono on Jesus," Patheos, October 3, 2016, https://tinyurl.com/ohdf8zy.

perpetrators) of evil will be transformed and redeemed. These prophecies imagine a possible world to live *into*, inviting us and challenging us to make the world better. These prophetic songs are idealistic in the best sense of the word. Like great works of art, they paint an ideal for us, inviting us to imagine what the world could be through what Martin Luther King Jr. once described as "the tireless effort and persistent work of [people] willing to be co-workers with God."[11]

These ancient songs express the range of human emotions—from hope to rage. The prophet Isaiah sings about the wicked war makers being slain, which, if taken literally, is vengeful. As a work of lyrical art, however, Isaiah's song resembles more modern songs like Bob Dylan's "Masters of War," which angrily accuses those who support the war industry of using death to make a profit. There will be no forgiveness for them, says Dylan. Isaiah and Dylan are singing similar songs, even though one is in the Bible and the other occupies a place in a different sort of canon. The same is true if we compare the prophetic songs of the prophet Amos with, say, Pink Floyd's "On the Turning Away." Both sing about hope and justice. Amos hopes for the day when justice will roll down like water; Pink Floyd hopes for the day when no one will ignore or turn away from those who suffer but will instead accept that we are all human beings who share the same planet.

Dylan's rage, Pink Floyd's dream, the example of Jesus, the visions of Isaiah and Amos—each is a work of art that expresses emotion, invigorates the imagination, opens our eyes to see suffering and evil around us, helps us dream of ways to make the world better, and then inspires us to work to realize that dream.

---

11. Martin Luther King Jr., "Letter from Birmingham Jail," Stanford University, April 16, 1963, https://tinyurl.com/je2l2rg.

Elisabeth Schüssler Fiorenza has written extensively about this progressive vision for "a different world of justice and well-being."[12] Schüssler Fiorenza sees this progressive dream embodied in the life of Jesus. Jesus, she says, lived the kingdom (or realm) of God, a kingdom that "envisions an alternative world free of hunger, poverty, and domination. This 'envisioned' world is already anticipated in [Jesus's] inclusive table-sharing, in the healing and liberating practices, as well as in the domination-free kinship community of the Jesus movement, which found many followers among the poor, the despised, the ill and possessed, the outcasts, prostitutes, and sinners."[13]

Progressive Christianity—which describes Jesus's ministry with utopian language, draws from art and song lyrics, speaks of dreams and visions, emphasizes compassion, expands the imagination, and inspires social action—has ancient roots. In this book, I will make a case for progressive Christianity that is informed by theology, tradition, history, philosophy, cultural anthropology, and careful exegesis of the Bible. It's a perspective on Christianity that treats the Bible and Christian tradition as compelling conversation *starters*.

The time is ripe for such a perspective. Americans now more than ever are open to progressive religion. While we still cling to religious traditions, we are becoming more socially liberal. The 2014 Pew Religious Landscape Study found that a staggering 83 percent of Americans are certain or fairly certain that there is a God, and another 6 percent are open to the

---

12. Elisabeth Schüssler Fiorenza, *Rhetoric and Ethic: The Politics of Biblical Studies* (Minneapolis: Fortress, 1999), 52.

13. Elisabeth Schüssler Fiorenza, *Jesus and the Politics of Interpretation* (New York: Continuum, 2001), 170.

possibility that there is a God.[14] At the same time, 69 percent of Americans believe abortion should remain legal in the United States, 62 percent believe humans evolved over time, and 62 percent say homosexuality should be accepted (this number has risen since 2014). Fewer than a third of Americans believe the Bible should be interpreted literally, nearly 60 percent call themselves politically moderate or liberal, nearly 80 percent say that religion is important or somewhat important in their lives, and 69 percent claim to regularly or fairly regularly attend religious services (from several times per month to a few times per year).

These look like glass-half-full numbers to me. I see an opportunity in this Pew survey, an infrastructure for building a progressive faith. Americans are sympathetic to the existence of God, skeptical of a literal interpretation of the Bible, socially progressive, and open to science and feel that religion is generally important in their lives. According to the Public Religion Research Institute, there is even strong evidence that religious progressives will soon outnumber religious conservatives in our country—a trend that's a breath of fresh air for many of us.[15] Moreover, we are living in what scholars such as Diana Butler Bass and others have argued is "a time of awakening" in our country.[16] The term *awakening* is deliberately used by these scholars to evoke the three Great Awakenings in the United States, one in each century beginning in the 1700s. Many

---

14. "Religious Landscape Study: Belief in God," Pew Research Center, June 4–September 30, 2014, http://www.pewforum.org/religious-landscape-study/.

15. See the explanation in Jonathan Merritt, "The Rise of the Christian Left in America," *Atlantic*, July 25, 2013, https://tinyurl.com/y8lmvuhu.

16. Diana Butler Bass, *Christianity after Religion: The End of Church and the Birth of a New Spiritual Awakening* (New York: HarperOne, 2012), 31.

believe we are now in the midst of a Fourth Great Awakening. Butler Bass summarizes,

> The First Great Awakening marked the end of European styles of church organization and created an experiential, democratic, pan-Protestant community of faith called evangelicalism. The Second Great Awakening ended Calvinist theological dominance and initiated new understandings of free will that resulted in a voluntary system for church membership and benevolent work. And the Third Great Awakening had two distinctive manifestations: the social gospel movement, with its progressive politics, and the Pentecostal movement, with an emphasis on miraculous transformation. . . . In each of these three awakenings, older forms of Christian faith . . . were revitalized, reoriented, remade, and sometimes replaced by more culturally resonant conceptions of self, God, community, and service to the world.[17]

What of the present-day Fourth Great Awakening? Butler Bass writes,

> The Fourth Great Awakening . . . moves into the heart of the world, facing the challenges head-on to take what is old—failed institutions, scarred landscapes, wearied religions, a wounded planet—and make them workable and humane in the service of the global community. No miracles here. God does not heal without human hands. The hard work is the possibility. [It] begins with the self-in-relationship, not the isolated hero, but the individual whose

---

17. Butler Bass, 29–30.

> life is linked with other heroic lives in a quest for beauty
> and justice and love. . . . The goal is to perform the reign [or
> Kingdom] of God in and for the life of the world.[18]

At the heart of this awakening is a progressive vision of the world. Its focus is on personal and institutional transformation for the benefit of "the global community." Its theology about the realm (or kingdom) of God is meant to enrich "the life of the world." Butler Bass and others have argued that this new awakening is unlike previous ones in that its borders extend beyond Christianity. The fourth awakening is an interfaith phenomenon. There are "profound transformations in every religious context," she writes. "These multiple spiritual awakenings are parallel events across faith boundaries."[19] And our awareness of religious diversity enables us to appreciate and draw from the wisdom of many traditions.

In my church in Ithaca, we have held contemplative prayer services that blend meditative practices from various faith traditions. I have conducted several interfaith services with clergy from other faith traditions in Ithaca. None of this means that we cease to be distinctively Christian or that we are watering down our tradition. It means that we appreciate that our tradition exists alongside others in a world of religious diversity. Theologian William Placher once noted that "important truths" can be learned from other religious traditions and, further, that even as one remains committed to a particular tradition, it is critical to "acknowledge that the truth one holds is only partial, that others have hold of real truths too, and that one can learn from

---

18. Butler Bass, 239.
19. Butler Bass, 244.

them in ways that will lead to correcting one's own position."[20] An image I often use when teaching confirmation classes at my church is that of a rainbow. I invite my teenage confirmands to think of the religions of the world as colors of a rainbow. Each one shines brighter when its adherents live more fully *into* their own traditions, even as they recognize and appreciate the beauty of the other colors.

Such progressive openness to diversity is consistent with what the Franciscan friar Richard Rohr argues in his book *The Universal Christ*. Rohr imagines that "future generations will label the first two thousand years of Christianity as 'early Christianity,'" in part, he says, because Christians both now and in the future will continue to recognize and privilege the universalistic aspects of our own tradition. Christ for us, argues Rohr, is a "universal Christ" who helps us see the divine imprint on all people, in all religious traditions, and in all creation—an insight that has biblical precedent:[21] "Christ is all and in all!" exclaims the writer of Colossians (Col 3:11). Foundational Christian claims about Christ from the past crack open the door to celebrating the diverse religious rainbow of the present and future. Christian tradition—our distinctive color on the rainbow—is a heritage that secures and anchors us; it is a deep well that we draw from as a place to start when considering how to engage with the world and address the pressing issues of our day.

I was reminded of the importance of having this sense of rootedness when I came across an interesting opinion piece that appeared in the *New York Times* on Easter Sunday in 2017 by the

---

20. William C. Placher, *Narratives of a Vulnerable God: Christ, Theology, and Scripture* (Louisville, KY: Westminster John Knox, 1994), 124.

21. Richard Rohr, *The Universal Christ: How a Forgotten Reality Can Change Everything We See, Hope for, and Believe* (London: SPCK, 2019), 48.

conservative Catholic columnist Ross Douthat. Douthat urged his readers to "give mainline Protestantism another chance" because, he said, "more religion would make liberalism more intellectually coherent."[22] Douthat is no liberal, but he wrote in defense of a thoughtful and well-grounded liberalism:

> Liberals, give mainline Protestantism another chance. Do it for your political philosophy: More religion would make liberalism more intellectually coherent. . . . Do it for your friends and neighbors, town and cities: Thriving congregations have spillover effects. . . . Do it for your family: Church is good for health and happiness, . . . and even its most modernized form is still an ark of memory, a link between the living and the dead. I understand that there's the minor problem of actual belief. But honestly, dear liberals, many of you *do* believe in the kind of open Gospel that a lot of mainline churches preach. If pressed, most of you aren't hard-core atheists: You pursue religious experiences, you have affinities for Unitarianism or Quakerism, you can even appreciate Christian orthodoxy when it's woven into Marilynne Robinson novels or the "Letter From Birmingham Jail." You say you're spiritual but not religious because you associate "religion" with hierarchies and dogmas and strict rules about sex. But the Protestant mainline has gone well out of its way to accommodate you on all these points.[23]

I agree with Douthat and would encourage everyone to give mainline progressive Protestantism another chance.

---

22. Ross Douthat, "Save the Mainline," *New York Times*, April 15, 2017, https://tinyurl.com/y6ouqsd5.
23. Douthat.

We have a saying in my denomination: "No matter who you are or where you are on life's journey, you are welcome here." The power of these words was hammered home for me not long ago when I went to lunch with a friend and her wife after they had visited our church. Both of them glowed after the service because, in their words, "*all* of them" was welcomed and accepted. Other people have expressed this same feeling to me, some of them clergy colleagues of mine. "All" for my friends meant not just that they were welcomed as visitors to the church but that they were welcomed as happily married lesbian visitors to the church. They saw the rainbow flag on our lawn, heard the welcome we speak every Sunday—"no matter who you are or where you are on life's journey, you are welcome here"—and knew that *all* of them, their *entire* selves, would be accepted and embraced.

On Sundays in my church, we always speak the "no matter who you are or where you are" UCC words of welcome, but we occasionally incorporate words of welcome from other churches. One time we borrowed words from Coventry Cathedral in England. National Public Radio (NPR) reported on Coventry's welcome, and when I heard the story on the radio, I immediately googled the church to access a written copy of the words.[24] The following Sunday in our service, we adapted Coventry's welcome for our congregation and its visitors. Here is what I read at the beginning of our service:

> We extend a special welcome to those who are single, married, divorced, widowed, straight, gay, confused, well-heeled, or down-at-heel. We especially welcome wailing babies and

---

24. "English Cathedral Welcomes Visitors with Unexpected Message," *Weekend Edition Sunday*, NPR, January 15, 2017, https://tinyurl.com/y5ntxd9l.

excited toddlers. We welcome you whether you can sing like Pavarotti or just growl quietly to yourself. You're welcome here if you're just browsing, just woken up, or just got out of prison. We don't care if you're more Christian than the Archbishop of Canterbury or haven't been to church since Christmas ten years ago. We extend a special welcome to those who are over sixty but not grown up yet and to teenagers who are growing up too fast. We welcome keep-fit moms, football dads, starving artists, tree huggers, latte sippers, vegetarians, junk food eaters. We welcome those who are in recovery or still addicted. We welcome you if you're having problems, are down in the dumps, or don't like organized religion. . . . We offer welcome to those who . . . work too hard, [are stressed out, tired out, down in the dumps, celebrating birthdays or anniversaries.] . . . We welcome those who are inked, pierced, both, or neither. We offer a special welcome to those who could use a prayer right now, had religion shoved down their throats as kids, or got lost [in our neighborhood] and wound up here by mistake. We welcome pilgrims, tourists, [visitors to one of our colleges], seekers, doubters, and you. [No matter who you are or where you are on life's journey, you are welcome here]

In this book, I will provide reasons why we believe that being progressive followers of Jesus requires that we open our arms wide and embrace everyone in this way. We have good reasons for being liberal and for calling ourselves progressive Christians, one of which is that being rooted and anchored to a tradition helps us avoid illiberalism. Douthat warns that "liberal Protestantism without the Protestantism tends to gradually shed the liberalism as well, transforming into an illiberal cult of victimologies that burns heretics with vigor. The wider experience of American politics suggests that as liberalism de-churches it struggles to find [an] . . . organizing principle, a persuasive language of the common good."[25] Douthat is referring here to a kerfuffle at Middlebury College in early 2017, which left Professor Allison Stanger in the hospital and was roundly condemned by academics, pundits, and parents of every political stripe.[26] In her opinion piece published two weeks after the event, Professor Stanger recounted what happened:

> I am the Middlebury College professor who ended up with whiplash and a concussion [after] . . . Charles Murray, a scholar at the American Enterprise Institute [visited my campus]. Though he is someone with whom I disagree, I welcomed the opportunity to moderate a talk with him on campus on March 2 because several of my students asked me to do so. . . . This was a chance to demonstrate publicly a commitment to a free and fair exchange of views in my classroom. But Dr. Murray was drowned out by students who never let him speak, and he and I were attacked and intimidated while trying to leave campus. In the days after the violence, some have spun this story as one about what's wrong with elite colleges and universities, our coddled youth or intolerant liberalism. Those analyses are incomplete. Political life and discourse in the United States is at a boiling point, and nowhere is the reaction to that more heightened than on college campuses. . . . That is the context

---

25. Douthat, "Save the Mainline."

26. See, for example, the joint statement by Princeton University professors Robert P. George and Cornell West, "Sign the Statement: Truth Seeking, Democracy, and Freedom of Thought and Expression—a Statement by Robert P. George and Cornell West," James Madison Program in American Ideals and Institutions, March 14, 2017, http://jmp.princeton.edu/statement.

into which Dr. Murray walked. . . . From the stage where I sat with Dr. Murray, waiting for students to take their seats, I saw a sea of humanity. Students were chanting, . . . yelling obscenities at Dr. Murray or [at] one another, . . . [and they] succeeded in shutting down the lecture. We were forced to move to another site and broadcast our discussion via live stream, while activists who had figured out where we were banged on the windows and set off fire alarms. Afterward, as Dr. Murray and I left the building with Bill Burger, Middlebury's vice president for communications, a mob charged us. Most of the hatred was focused on Dr. Murray, but when I took his right arm to shield him and to make sure we stayed together, the crowd turned on me. Someone pulled my hair, while others were shoving me. I feared for my life. Once we got into the car, protesters climbed on it, hitting the windows and rocking the vehicle whenever we stopped to avoid harming them. I am still wearing a neck brace, and spent a week in a dark room to recover from a concussion caused by the whiplash.[27]

Besides being a terrifying example of what Douthat calls illiberal behavior in an elite institution of higher education in America, this episode illustrated for me what an anchorless, rootless, and even bankrupted form of itself liberalism can become. It can become bitter and bad without the organizing principle of a deep tradition that can provide a sense of history

---

27. Allison Stanger, "Understanding the Angry Mob at Middlebury That Gave Me a Concussion," *New York Times*, March 13, 2017, https://tinyurl.com/yyp3rw84.

and a moral compass. As Douthat puts it, "Liberal Protestantism without the Protestantism tends to gradually shed the liberalism as well."[28]

The riot at Middlebury College is significant in my view because it raises the *why* question. *Why* might we progressives think that someone like Charles Murray is wrong? The immediate urge of feeling offended by him and by what he has written and said—as repulsive and abhorrent as they are—is not sufficient to justify shutting him down in the way that Professor Stanger describes. A robust prophetic tradition of nonviolent protest exists within progressive Christianity, manifested most clearly in the civil rights movement. This tradition of progressive Christianity focuses on people's rights and social justice not because *rights* and *justice* are buzzwords that nicely adorn a placard but because these words are rooted in a deep and ancient tradition that proclaims the intrinsic worth of every person. Progressive Christians believe that each person has been fashioned by God in God's own image and is thus priceless in the eyes of a mothering God who loves her children. She loves the world's protesting college students as well as the world's Charles Murrays. The gospel she would have us proclaim by word and deed is not merely one that announces inclusive love; it is also a gospel with teeth. It is a gospel that bites. The gospel, as Jesus once put it, is "good news to the poor," "release to the captives," "sight to the blind," and freedom for "the oppressed" (Luke 4:18–19). It is not a rootless liberalism or a reactionary, soulless materialism. It is ancient, robust, thoughtful, grounded, compassionate, spiritually rich, justice oriented, and challenging. It is an organizing principle. It is a

---

28. Douthat, "Save the Mainline."

global vision of liberation, articulated so beautifully in one of my favorite hymns, "Canticle of the Turning" by Rory Cooney. Drawn from Mary's Magnificat in the Gospel of Luke, this hymn is a cry to God for justice, for the removal of tyrannical leaders, for the filling of hungry bellies, and for the hammering of implements of war into farming tools, and it expresses the ancient prophetic hope that the world is about to turn.

2

OF GOD AND BUBBLES

Speaking of God is never speaking of God but only ever speaking about our understanding of God.
> —Peter Rollins, *How (Not) to Speak of God*

The kind of God in whom one believes has implications for the kind of life one tries to live.
> —William C. Placher, *Narratives of a Vulnerable God*

My idea of God is not a divine idea. It has to be shattered time after time. He shatters it Himself. He is the great iconoclast.
> —C. S. Lewis, *A Grief Observed*

It is in fact absurd and impossible to try to grasp God as an object which can be seized and comprehended by our minds.
> —Thomas Merton, *Contemplative Prayer*

Talk about God: theology has been growing uncertain for centuries. Therein lies its great opportunity.
> —Catherine Keller, *Face of the Deep*

FOUCAULT, MEANING, AND GOD

In a little book titled *This Is Not a Pipe*, philosopher Michel Foucault analyzes René Magritte's painting *La trahison des images* (*The Treachery of Images*).[1] The surrealist painting depicts a pipe, under which reads the caption "Ceci n'est pas une pipe" (This is not a pipe). Viewers of the painting know that the pipe is not literally a pipe but rather a drawing of one. But if we already intuitively know this, then why is there a caption telling us that this is not a pipe? The caption seems redundant unless it is referring not to the drawing of the pipe but to something else. Foucault plays with this ambiguity. It could be that the caption is referring to itself, as if to say, "I am not a pipe but a sentence that says that I am not a pipe." Or it could be that the caption is referring to the entire painting, as if to say, "This painting that depicts a pipe and the sentence 'This is not a pipe' is *not* a pipe." Magritte's painting and Foucault's analysis of it illustrate a fundamental problem with connecting words on a page—or a painting—to a thing. Elsewhere in his writings, Foucault traces the histories of ideas like madness, sexuality, and the punishment of criminals to argue that such words and phrases do not correspond to stable things but to things that mean different things at different times.

The meaning of the word *God* is likewise unstable. We live in a time when the role of God in our world is different than it was for our forebears centuries ago. Once, folk might nod in agreement at a comment made by sixteenth-century Reformer John Calvin: "Some mothers have full and abundant breasts, but others' are almost dry, as God wills to feed one [infant] more

---

1. Michel Foucault, *This Is Not a Pipe*, ed. and trans. James Harkness (Berkeley: University of California Press, 2008).

liberally, but another more meagerly."[2] But for most of us today, such a comment sounds absurd, even morally obtuse.

According to Homer's *Iliad*, the anger of the god Apollo was responsible for crippling the Achaean army with a plague as it camped on the shores of Troy. We question today whether the Trojan War took place in the way Homer describes, and almost no one would attribute an army's success or failure on the battlefield to the intervention of Greek gods.

Religious behavior was once regulated by touching a stone on which were engraved various rules of conduct. By touching the stone, religious practitioners were publicly stating that their conduct was pure. On the stone was a warning, however, that touching it would expose a naughty person to the wrath of the gods.[3] (I am referring here to the archaeological discovery of a stone with an inscription about a religion practiced in the house of a man named Dionysios around the year 100 BCE in the ancient city of Philadelphia in the region of Lydia. I'll return to this inscription in chapter 5.) Most people today don't believe in magic rocks.

According to Reza Aslan, our prehistoric ancestors once knelt in devotion before sacred trees believed to talk and even move (a bit like Ents in Tolkien's *Lord of the Rings* trilogy).[4] It is safe to say that for most of us today, trees may be deemed

---

2. Calvin, *Institutes of the Christian Religion* I.xvi.3, 200–201.

3. Richard S. Ascough, Philip A. Harland, and John S. Kloppenborg, eds., *Associations in the Greco-Roman World: A Sourcebook* (Waco, TX: Baylor University Press, 2012), 82–84: "The gods will be merciful to those who obey and will always give them all good things, whatever things gods give to people whom they love. But if any transgress, the gods will hate such people and inflict upon them great punishments. . . . May those men and women who have confidence in themselves touch this stone on which the instructions of the god have been written, so that those who obey these instructions and those who do not obey these instructions may become evident."

4. Reza Aslan, *God: A Human History* (New York: Random House, 2017).

special or even sacred as a part of creation, but not because they can walk or talk.

For a growing number of people today, God is not relevant to daily life and has thus become an unemployed deity fit to be tossed into history's dustbin. Christopher Hitchens quipped that his friend Salman Rushdie had criticized the title of a book Hitchens wrote, *God Is Not Great*. Rushdie said the title was "exactly one word too long" and that it should have been titled *God Is Not*.[5] In 1966, *Time* magazine published a cover with a question in bold, red lettering: "Is God dead?" This provocative question emerged at the height of the so-called Death of God movement in the theology of the 1960s. By "death," people have meant various things. For some, God actually died on the cross with Jesus (the cry "My God, my God, why have you forsaken me?" was a moment, writes G. K. Chesterton, when "God seemed for an instant to be an atheist"[6]). For others, God is irrelevant to the lives of modern human beings and so is, for all intents and purposes, *dead* to us. Though it is tempting to mordantly ask with Catherine Keller and Laurel C. Schneider "just *which* God it is that is presumed dead,"[7] given the plurality of theologies and views of God in our time, it is important to realize that the movement that led to the *Time* cover was made possible by many developments in the modern world: Charles Darwin and evolution by natural selection; our expanding knowledge of the cosmos and our insignificant place in it; the realization that nuclear weapons have enabled human beings to destroy the world; the haunting memories of the Holocaust

---

5. Christopher Hitchens, *Hitch-22: A Memoir* (New York: Twelve, 2010), 9.

6. G. K. Chesterton, *Orthodoxy* (New York: Snowball Classics, 2015), 90.

7. Catherine Keller and Laurel C. Schneider, introduction to *Polydoxy: Theology of Multiplicity and Relation* (London: Routledge, 2011), 1.

(Where was God in all of that suffering?); Karl Marx's argument that material (i.e., economic) forces, not divine ones, drive human behavior; Sigmund Freud's argument that God is a projection of our childish desire for a father figure's protection; and Friedrich Nietzsche's Madman, the atheistic prophet who announced that God is dead, that he remains dead, and that we are the ones who have killed him. By proclaiming that the idea of God (and Christian morality) no longer controls human destiny, Nietzsche, writes Terry Eagleton, "has a strong claim to being the first real atheist" in Western history.[8]

The list goes on and on. Climate change, terrorism, economic crises, human trafficking, global pandemics—each one, like another brick mortared to Pink Floyd's wall, causes many of our contemporaries to feel adrift, walled off, and separated from God. The God concept seems no longer to work for many of us. Philosopher Peter Sloterdijk describes the death of God and its bleak effect:

It deals with the meaning of losing the cosmic periphery, the collapse of the metaphysical immune system that had stabilized . . . Old European thought. . . . What this actually means is that the orb is dead, the containing circle has burst, . . . and our faith in God on high, without whom not a single hair on a mortal head had fallen out until yesterday, has become powerless, groundless and hopeless; for the height is empty, the edge no longer holds the world together, and the picture has fallen out of its divine frame. And with

---

8. Terry Eagleton, *Culture and the Death of God* (New Haven, CT: Yale University Press, 2014), 151.

this picture, humans too must drift away from the framework of their faith and can henceforth only exist as if in free fall.[9]

But the "death of God" says nothing about whether God exists but says much about how many of our contemporaries *experience* God (or God's absence). To say God exists or God does not exist is to make a statement of either faith or faith's absence. To live in what Sloterdijk calls "shelless times" is to experience the feeling that there is no protective God watching over us.[10] It is not unlike the experience of the writer of Ecclesiastes, whose somber biblical text dips its toes into the waters of shelless times: "Again I saw that under the sun the race is not to the swift, nor the battle to the strong, nor bread to the wise, nor riches to the intelligent, nor favor to the skillful; but *time and chance happen to them all*. For no one can anticipate the time of disaster. Like fish taken in a cruel net, and like birds caught in a snare, so mortals are snared at a time of calamity, when it suddenly falls upon them" (Eccl 9:11–12; italics mine). Ecclesiastes is a voice of skepticism in the chorus of Scripture; the death of God is a modern experience (with some ancient precursors) among many other experiences that people have *of* God.

And yet in spite of changing views toward God today, and in spite of the fact that God is irrelevant (or dead) for many people, according to the Pew Research Center, 89 percent of Americans either believe in God or are sympathetic to the idea of God.[11] "God is [for most of us] too vital a piece of ideology to

---

9. Peter Sloterdijk, *Spheres*, vol. 2, *Globes, Macrospherology*, trans. Wieland Hoban (South Pasadena, CA: Semiotext[e], 2014), 559.

10. Peter Sloterdijk, *Spheres*, vol. 1, *Bubbles, Microspherology*, trans. Wieland Hoban (South Pasadena, CA: Semiotext[e], 2011), 26.

11. "Religious Landscape Study."

be [completely] written off," writes Eagleton.[12] But the question is, What do we mean when we say the word *God*? To what, if anything, does the word *God* refer?

GOD AND SCRIPTURE

Answering this question with the Bible as a starting point is complicated by the fact that God in Scripture is a composite figure, an amalgamation of personalities borrowed from various ancient deities, as scholars Mark Smith, Jack Miles, and others have pointed out.[13] God as a warrior and controller of the weather mirrors attributes of the ancient Canaanite deity Baal. God as a high god and the head of a divine council mirrors attributes of the ancient Near East high god El. God as a warrior in the Old Testament (Hebrew Bible) mirrors attributes ascribed to Chemosh by the Moabite king Mesha. His words are preserved in an inscription called the Mesha Stele: "And Chemosh said to me: 'Go, take Nebo from Israel!' And I went in the night, and I fought against it from the break of dawn until noon, and I took it, and I killed its whole population, seven thousand male citizens and aliens, female citizens and aliens, and servant girls. . . . And the king of Israel had built Jahaz, and he stayed there during his campaigns against me, and Chemosh drove him away before my face."[14] Even the Christian Christmas story about God being miraculously conceived

---

12. Eagleton, *Culture and Death of God*, 151.

13. See Mark S. Smith, *The Early History of God: Yahweh and the Other Deities in Ancient Israel* (Grand Rapids, MI: Eerdmans, 2002); and Jack Miles, *God: A Biography* (New York: Vintage, 1995).

14. William Brown, "Moabite Stone [Mesha Stele]," Ancient History Encyclopedia, February 11, 2019, https://tinyurl.com/y2895jgl.

draws from the ancient Greco-Roman notion that heroes and wonder-workers needed to be from the gods (i.e., miraculously conceived) in order to be objects of veneration.

God is a complicated and composite figure in Scripture, but speaking about the *thing* called God is also complicated by personal factors as well. Theologian Catherine Keller has noted that "we bring so much baggage to the concept of 'God' that we can hardly move, let alone undertake a journey."[15] My own journey with the concept of God has been labyrinthine—into and out of several "death of God" experiences. I have expended much intellectual energy on my journey of faith struggling to understand God within a balanced system. I have since learned that the words *system* and *balance* are ill-suited for the topic of God in the Bible and in our sacred tradition. God in the Bible is less like the rolling mellifluous fluency of, say, Antonio Vivaldi's *Nisi Dominus* and more like the cacophonic jazz-classical-electronic sound one hears from a band like the Necks or like the blending of violent rage and symphonic beauty in the early and later albums of the metal band Mastodon.

Years ago, when I was still an evangelical Christian, I considered myself to be a Reformed Calvinist, trusting in the absolute sovereignty of God as a king in the sky. Calvinism's depiction of God is part of a branch of Christian theology that first emerged in the writings of Saint Augustine in the fifth century CE but that came to full blossom in what was eventually known as the Five Points of Calvinism, summarized with the acrostic *TULIP*: Total depravity (humanity is hopelessly ensnared in sin and separated from God), Unconditional election (God, out of sheer grace, has chosen to save a portion—an "elect"—out

---

15. Catherine Keller, *On the Mystery: Discerning Divinity in Process* (Minneapolis: Fortress, 2008), x.

of the mass of a lost humanity), *Limited* atonement (God sent Christ to die on the cross to save this limited, elect number and no one else), *Irresistible* grace (God's spirit miraculously regenerates the elect so that they willingly exercise faith, which is itself a gift of God's grace), *Perseverance* of the saints (God will miraculously preserve the elect and take them to heaven when they die; they cannot lose their salvation because they have been chosen by God).

TULIP is a neatly organized system. Predictable and secure. But all theologies that try to systematize God and God's work in the world, whether those birthed centuries ago such as Calvinism or more recent attempts such as process theology, are human-made constructs. They are systems that *produce* images of God. Or put differently, they are systems filled with *words* that may or may not correspond to the *thing* called God.

The break from what I sometimes call my first language of faith in Calvinism was clinched when I decided to read the Bible from cover to cover in one year with the goal of recording every single action of God in a little orange notebook. That notebook is filled with chapter and verse lists of all of God's actions from every book in the Bible. Reading and recording everything God does in the Bible from January 1 to December 31 changed my life of faith. I not only discovered that God is not a uniform concept in the Bible; I discovered that the concept of God is flat-out contradictory. It does not fit seamlessly into a system; it is not balanced.

Years later, as a recovering evangelical, I taught a seminar course at St. Olaf College called "The Biblical God." This was a theology course, but I stayed in my wheelhouse as a Scripture scholar—a scholar of texts—and had my students do projects that required them to read the Bible closely and compare the ways in which God is presented in various passages. One assignment asked students to compare everything God or the Angel of the Lord says or does in the Old Testament book of Judges with everything God, Jesus, or the Spirit says or does in the New Testament letter of Second Thessalonians. (I honestly can't remember why I chose these two biblical books to assign my students. It seemed like a good idea at the time.)

My students had to provide a detailed chart comparing the two books and then write a substantial paper analyzing and drawing conclusions from the data they collected. When it came time for them to evaluate the course, this assignment ranked at the top of the list of the most memorable because students appreciated the challenge of dealing with Scripture at the microlevel of words and images of God. They got down into the weeds of Scripture, rooting around in portions of individual verses, digging out snippets of phrases that, as some feminist theologians say, render God. The eye-opening aspect of the assignment for my students was the same as it had been for me as I filled in my little orange notebook: God in Scripture comes across as very human at times, even petty, with dirty fingernails from rifling around in human messes and bloody hands from fighting wars. *He* (almost always a he!) is not the regally elegant and bearded European male that one finds in, say, Michelangelo's depiction of God on the Sistine Chapel's ceiling. God is not Renaissance-type clean in Scripture, though such a Renaissance-type clean image of God helped make possible rectilinear theological systems like TULIP, which are, admittedly, well manicured in their own high baroque sorts of ways.

To be sure, great beauty can be found in the ways many biblical texts portray God. God is love (1 John 4:8); God is a comforting mother (Isa 66:13); God is a prodigal father who rushes out to embrace and kiss his wayward children when they return home (Luke 15:20–24); God's presence fills the whole earth (Jer 23:24); God is a gentle shepherd (Ps 23), a covering shade (Ps 121:5), a refuge and strength (Ps 46:1), a kind king (Ps 47), and a fortress (Ps 62:6). Revelation uses dazzling imagery to express God's hope that the world will one day be peaceful like a sea of glass (Rev 15:2). And few places in Scripture can match the lyrical wonder of the songwriter who sings about God in Psalm 146. Robert Alter offers a straightforward translation of this song that preserves the simplicity of the Hebrew poetry:

> Happy whose help is Jacob's God
> his hope—for the Lord his God,
> maker of heaven and earth,
> the sea, and of all that is in them;
> Who keeps faith forever,
> does justice for the oppressed,
> gives bread to the hungry,
> the Lord looses those in fetters.
> The Lord gives sight to the blind.
> The Lord makes the bent stand erect.
> The Lord loves the righteous.
> The Lord guards sojourners,
> orphan and widow He sustains.[16] (Ps 146:5–9a)

These texts describe God as tender, powerful, loving, gracious, and deeply concerned for the down-and-out, the poor, the prisoners, the strangers, the hungry, and the oppressed. They speak of God with language that reminds me of a prayer from Alexander Carmichael's *Carmina Gadelica*:

---

16. Robert Alter, *The Book of Psalms: A Translation with Commentary* (New York: W. W. Norton, 2007), 503–4.

A shade art thou in the heat.
A shelter art thou in the cold.
Eyes art thou to the blind.
A staff art thou to the pilgrim.
An island art thou at sea.
A fortress art thou on land.
A well art thou in the desert.
Health art thou to the ailing.[17]

These beautiful voices that form a chorus are not the only ones in Scripture, however. "The Bible speaks not with one voice but with many," writes scholar Michael Coogan, and "the different voices are not always in harmony."[18] There are many places in the Bible where God gets messy. Indeed, the word *God* in Scripture is sometimes used to justify terrible actions, the very worst of humanity. God, or "the Lord [Yahweh]," in Scripture directly orders people to spill blood or approvingly nods when humans engage in such violence. For example, the golden calf incident in Exodus 32 portrays both God and Moses as condoning vengeful slaughter:

When Moses saw that the people were running wild . . . , [he] stood in the gate of the camp, and said, "Who is on the Lord's side? Come to me!" And all the sons of Levi gathered around him. He said to them, "*Thus says the Lord, the God of Israel,* 'Put your sword on your side, each of you! Go back and forth from gate to gate throughout the camp, and each of you kill your brother, your friend, and your neighbor.'" The sons of

---

17. Quoted in Kenneth McIntosh, *Water from an Ancient Well: Celtic Spirituality for Modern Life* (Vestal, NY: Anamchara Books, 2011), 293.

18. Michael Coogan, *The Old Testament: A Very Short Introduction* (New York: Oxford University Press, 2008), 110, 123.

Levi did as Moses commanded, and about three thousand of the people fell on that day. Moses said, "Today you have ordained yourselves for the service of the Lord, each one at the cost of a son or a brother, and so have brought a blessing on yourselves this day." On the next day Moses said to the people, "You have sinned a great sin. But now I will go up to the Lord; perhaps I can make atonement for your sin." So Moses returned to the Lord and said, "Alas, this people has sinned a great sin; they have made for themselves gods of gold. But now, if you will only forgive their sin. . . ." *But the Lord said* to Moses, "Whoever has sinned against me I will blot out of my book. But now go, lead the people to the place about which I have spoken to you; see, my angel shall go in front of you. . . ." Then *the Lord sent* a plague on the people, because they made the calf. (Exod 32:25–35; italics mine)

Peter Sloterdijk says this is "one of the most terrible passages of all time in the whole of religious history" because it closely connects monotheism with violence, inaugurating a dark trajectory in history that sanctions wars as crusades and suicide bombings as martyrdom.[19] The phrase "Thus says the Lord, the God of Israel" justifies the violence that ensues. As with Michel Foucault's analysis of Magritte's painting of the pipe, there is ambiguity in these words because God is not the direct speaker. The command to strap on a sword and spill blood is spoken by Moses, but is Moses channeling God's words as a mouthpiece of the divine, or is he interpreting in his own words a command God had already given? Or, since Scripture accords Moses a

---

19. Peter Sloterdijk, *In the Shadow of Mount Sinai: A Footnote on the Origins and Changing Forms of Total Membership*, trans. Wieland Holan (Cambridge: Polity, 2016), 28.

special place among the prophets as the only one to speak with God "face to face" (see Num 12:7–8), perhaps Moses's words were the actual words of God. At the very least, the writer(s) of this story wielded the phrase "Thus says the Lord" as a rhetorical device to justify the massacre of three thousand people, even adding at the end of the story that "the Lord sent a plague" to further punish the people.

Divinely sanctioned killing in Scripture is unfortunately rather routine. God goes to war in the books of Joshua and Judges. In Joshua, after "Joshua fought the battle of Jericho and the walls came tumbling down," as we used to sing in Sunday school, Joshua orders the entire city to be put to the sword in God's name: "On the seventh day they rose early, at dawn, and marched around the city in the same manner seven times. It was only on that day that they marched around the city seven times. And at the seventh time, when the priests had blown the trumpets, Joshua said to the people, 'Shout! For *the Lord has given you the city*. The city and all that is in it shall be devoted to the Lord for destruction'" (Josh 6:15–17; italics mine). I don't remember this part of the story being included in that song we sang in Sunday school. Nor do I remember hearing as a child about the dead bodies washed up onto the shores of the Red Sea after the exodus:

> Then *the Lord said* to Moses, "Stretch out your hand over the sea, so that the water may come back upon the Egyptians, upon their chariots and chariot drivers." So Moses stretched out his hand over the sea, and at dawn the sea returned to its normal depth. As the Egyptians fled before it, *the Lord tossed* the Egyptians into the sea. The waters returned and covered the chariots and the chariot drivers, the entire army of Pharaoh that had followed them into the sea; not one of

them remained. But the Israelites walked on dry ground through the sea, the waters forming a wall for them on their right and on their left. Thus *the Lord saved Israel that day* from the Egyptians; and Israel saw the Egyptians dead on the seashore. (Exod 14:26–30; italics mine)

My students were especially surprised to read about the viciousness of God's warmongering in Judges: "Deborah said to Barak, 'Up! For this is the day on which *the Lord has given* Sisera into your hand. *The Lord is indeed going out before you.*' . . . *And the Lord threw* Sisera and all his chariots and all his army into a panic before Barak; Sisera got down from his chariot and fled away on foot. . . . All the army of Sisera fell by the sword; no one was left. . . . So on that day *God subdued* King Jabin of Canaan before the Israelites" (Judg 4:14–16, 23; italics mine). Elsewhere in Judges, they discovered that God not only fights wars but authorizes human sacrifice:

Then *the spirit of the Lord came upon* Jephthah, and he passed through Gilead and Manasseh. He passed on to Mizpah of Gilead, and from Mizpah of Gilead he passed on to the Ammonites. And Jephthah made a vow to the Lord, and said, "If you will give the Ammonites into my hand, then whoever comes out of the doors of my house to meet me, when I return victorious from the Ammonites, shall be the Lord's, to be offered up by me as a burnt offering." So Jephthah crossed over to the Ammonites to fight against them; and *the Lord gave them* into his hand. He inflicted a massive defeat on them from Aroer to the neighborhood of Minnith, twenty towns, and as far as Abel-keramim. So the Ammonites were subdued before the people of Israel. (Judg 11:29–33; italics mine)

The twist in this is that Jephthah's daughter, Mizpah, is the first to greet him at the doors of his house (Judg 11:34). The story is curiously cryptic about whether Mizpah was actually sacrificed (see v. 39), though it seems likely that she was and that God had condoned it. God is frequently portrayed in Judges as sanctioning morally questionable actions, whether working through armies to spill blood or sending an evil spirit to incite political treachery (Judg 9:23) or taking advantage of Samson's love of a Philistine woman as a pretext to fight a war with the Philistines (Judg 14:4) or strengthening Samson's arms so he could topple the pillars of the temple of Dagon, killing himself and three thousand Philistines (Judg 16:23–30).

God-ordained violence scars the Bible's pages from cover to cover. In Genesis, God rains down terror from the sky and wipes out the people of Sodom and Gomorrah: "Then *the Lord rained* on Sodom and Gomorrah sulfur and fire *from the Lord* out of heaven; and *he overthrew* those cities, and all the Plain, and all the inhabitants of the cities, and what grew on the ground" (Gen 19:24–25; italics mine). In First Samuel, God commands the Israelites to commit genocide: "Thus *says the Lord of hosts,* '*I will punish* the Amalekites for what they did in opposing the Israelites when they came up out of Egypt. Now go and attack Amalek, and utterly destroy all that they have; do not spare them, but kill both man and woman, child and infant, ox and sheep, camel and donkey'" (1 Sam 15:2–3; italics mine). In the Second Letter to the Thessalonians, the writer portrays God exercising retributive punishment "to repay with affliction" those who afflict the Thessalonian Christians, to inflict "vengeance on those who do not know God and on those who do not obey the gospel of our Lord Jesus" (2 Thess 1:6, 8). And Revelation contains the clearest example in the New Testament of using God to rationalize the morally abhorrent.

In Revelation 6, four horsemen—a rider on a white horse, a rider on a red horse, a rider on a black horse, and a rider on a pale green horse—are summoned before the throne of God and then sent out to wreak havoc on the earth, removing peace to ensure that swords can slay more successfully and hurling chaos to ensure that famine, pestilence, and wild beasts would wipe out a fourth of the human population.

There are dozens of similar examples throughout Scripture of God orchestrating human suffering and death. The Bible approves of all sorts of morally dubious and sometimes outright repulsive things in God's name. Its words have been used to condemn gay people (e.g., Lev 18:22; Rom 1:26–27), prohibit interracial and interreligious marriage (e.g., Ezra 9:1–10:14), tell wives to submit to their husbands as slaves to masters who beat them (e.g., 1 Pet 3:1–6 in a context of slaves and masters; cf. 1 Pet 2:18–20), order slaves to obey their masters (e.g., 1 Pet 2:18–20; Col 3:22; Eph 6:5–8), and promise that Jesus will one day appear as a rider on a white horse to splatter the blood of his enemies (e.g., Rev 19:11–16; 2 Thess 1:7–9; 2:8). The Bible is a big book that contains many bad things.

GOD AND ETHICS

The bad images of God that its pages contain get used by people to say and do terrible things in God's name: crusades, inquisitions, witch burnings, religious wars, slavery, and sundry forms of hate aimed at "others." A modern example is the "God hates fags" picketing campaign of the Westboro Baptist Church.[20]

---

20. Westboro Baptist Church (website), accessed February 26, 2021, http://www.godhatesfags.com/index.html.

Westboro members have shown up at the funerals of veterans, churches, government buildings, town squares, and university campuses holding signs with the words "God Hates Fags," "Thank God for AIDS," "Fag Troops," and "Fags Burn in Hell." Members once showed up at Cornell University with their repugnant signs to protest the university's diversity policy. My children were toddlers at the time, and I loaded them into their double stroller, adorned the stroller with the appropriate rainbow bling, donned my clerical garb, and joined a dozen other liberal clergies to lead a counterprotest in support of LGBTQ+ Cornell students. I am proud to say it was my children's first act of civic engagement.

Both God and the Bible are still being put to use by conservative Christians to justify the bizarre and unthinkable. On October 17, 2017, the *Huffington Post* recounted comments made by televangelist Jim Bakker:

> Jim Bakker has had it with his critics. The disgraced televangelist is demanding that "mean people in America" who make fun of him stop watching his show. . . . He's warning that there will be dire consequences for those who continue to watch and mock. "If you don't want to hear it, just shut me off," he said. . . . "Especially you folks that monitor me every day to try to destroy me." . . . Then he fired off this warning: "One day, you're going to shake your fist in God's face. And you're going to say, 'God, why didn't you warn me?' He's gonna say, 'You sat there and you made fun of Jim Bakker all those years. I warned you, but you didn't listen.'"[21]

---

21. Ed Mazza, "Jim Bakker Says God Will Punish You for Making Fun of Him," *Huffington Post*, October 17, 2017, https://tinyurl.com/ycuqjdvc.

Then on November 9, 2017, the *Washington Post* reported that Alabama state auditor Jim Zeigler was defending then GOP Senate candidate Roy Moore, who was accused of pedophilia, by pointing to Joseph and Mary in Scripture as an example of an older man courting a teenaged girl in order to justify Moore's behavior.[22] The responses to this outrageous comment were legion, but I especially appreciated William Barber's tweet: "For the record: the Bible teaches that Joseph married Mary & was faithful to her thru great trials. He didn't sexually assault her as a minor; he shielded her from shame & violence."[23]

A still more recent example of such theological malpractice occurred on September 23, 2019, when Robert Jeffress, senior minister of the First Baptist Church of Dallas and staunch supporter of Donald Trump, criticized teenage climate activist Greta Thunberg on a radio program, saying, "This Greta Thunberg, the sixteen-year-old, she was warning today about the mass extinction of humanity. Somebody needs to read poor Greta Genesis chapter 9 and tell her the next time she worries about global warming, just look at a rainbow; that's God's promise that the polar ice caps aren't going to melt and flood the world again."[24] Such twisted uses of God and the Bible in Christian history and more recently by members of the Westboro Baptist Church, Jim Bakker, Jim Ziegler, and Robert Jeffress are made possible in part by the Bible's own questionable morals when it

---

22. Michelle Boorstein, "Alabama State Official Defends Roy Moore, Citing Joseph and Mary: 'They Became Parents of Jesus,'" *Washington Post*, November 19, 2017, https://tinyurl.com/y6nhzbvq.

23. See, for example, Daniel Schultz, "Jesus, Mary, Joseph: The Disgusting Religious Defense of Roy Moore," *Religion Dispatches*, November 10, 2017, https://tinyurl.com/y5vbsffr.

24. "Todd Starnes and Dr. Robert Jeffress," Fox News, September 23, 2019, https://tinyurl.com/y4ynktnw.

comes to issues of human sexuality, gender roles, slavery, and especially the use of violence. Scholar of religion Bruce Lincoln points out that "religious discourse [i.e., God-talk] can recode virtually any content as sacred."[25] Lincoln explains that justifying violence in God's name is endemic not just to biblical religion but to all religions: "Confronted with the disquieting reality of religious conflict, popular wisdom typically comforts itself with the . . . refrain: 'How sad to see wars in the name of religion, when all religions preach peace.' However well intentioned such sentiments may be, they manage to ignore the fact that all religions sanction, even enjoin the use of violence under certain circumstances, the definitions of which have proven conveniently elastic."[26] As a pastor and scholar of religion myself, I fear that we put our heads in the sand if we try to deny this fact and push away the ethical responsibility we all share as religious practitioners of our own religious traditions.

In the Christian tradition, this means acknowledging the dark corners of our sacred text as well as resisting their glib dismissals: "The God of the Old Testament is not the same as the God of the New Testament," or worse, "Christianity is more advanced than Judaism." An antidote to such Marcionite platitudes can be found in Revelation, portions of Second Thessalonians, various quips in Paul's letters, the grim story of Ananias and Sapphira being struck dead at the words of the apostle Peter (Acts 5:1–11), the seething rage of Jesus about "weeping and gnashing of teeth" (e.g., Matt 13:42), as well as alarming scenes from extrabiblical Christian texts like the Acts of Peter—which imaginatively depicts Peter as a hero who supernaturally mutes

---

25. Bruce Lincoln, *Holy Terrors: Thinking about Religion after September 11* (Chicago: University of Chicago Press, 2006), 6.

26. Lincoln, 73.

the heresies of a competing hero named Simon Magus—or the Apocalypse of Paul, which details the medieval-like tortures of people in hell (complete with strangulations, hot irons, lacerations, rivers of fire, and snow).

The Bible and Christian tradition can be harrowing. The Bible and Christian tradition can also be stunningly beautiful. Both are a bit like Pablo Picasso's 1937 painting *Guernica*, which depicts the horrors of the Nazi bombing campaign in the city of Guernica in the Spanish province of Biscay. The painting is a blend of beauty and horror.

We readers of the Bible who call ourselves progressive Christians can freely admit the bad without losing sight of the ethical responsibility to affirm the good, especially in a world of Jim Bakker, Jim Zeigler, Robert Jeffress, and the Westboro Baptist Church—a world where "what the Bible says" is used as a bludgeon to pummel "others"; a world where, as Bryan Mealer writes, "the institution of Jesus Christ [the church] . . . has been co-opted by corporate interests, culture warriors, and the false religion of Fox News, just as it was by slavers and segregationists"; a world that desperately needs a clear progressive Christian alternative to the damaging use of the Bible by too many in our day.[27]

STRUGGLING WITH SCRIPTURE

In her landmark study of early Christian history *In Memory of Her*, Elisabeth Schüssler Fiorenza articulated a way to achieve

---

27. Bryan Mealer, "How I Became Christian Again: My Long Journey to Find Faith Once More," *Guardian*, December 25, 2017, https://tinyurl.com/y8ov7qta.

this end.[28] Writing from a feminist perspective, she describes interpreting the Bible as an act of struggle. Biblical texts do not preserve memories of what really happened in the past, nor do their words describe who God really is. As with Foucault and the painting of the pipe, the words on the page have an ambiguous relationship to the thing itself (whether a pipe or God). Biblical words tell us about *people's* experiences of the divine or the sacred (as scholar Mircea Eliade called it), not what the sacred *actually is*. The Bible preserves what *people once said* about God. Whether their words about God still resonate today is for *us* to decide in the context of our communities of faith.

Accordingly, progressive Bible readers are constantly struggling with Scripture, dialoguing with it, and feeling it out to see what speaks to them on their faith journeys. Progressive Bible interpreters and preachers who speak to and for communities of faith have an ethical responsibility to privilege those elements of biblical God-talk that highlight the best in God and God's relationship to people, especially society's most vulnerable: the poor, the immigrant, the oppressed, the gender nonconforming, and the hated. This means reading Scripture through the lens of Jesus's first sermon in Luke's Gospel, which proclaims that the best of God brings good news to the poor, releases all held captive, opens blind eyes, and sets the oppressed free (Luke 4:18). The gospel—the good news—proclaims liberation from sin, sadness, sickness, addiction, depression, abuse, trauma, injustice, and everything that binds people up and presses them down. Its light pierces shadows, exposing flickers of hope in a world of crosses.

---

28. Elisabeth Schüssler Fiorenza, *In Memory of Her: A Feminist Theological Reconstruction of Christian Origins* (New York: Crossroad, 2005).

Schüssler Fiorenza writes that interpretation "must uncover and reject those elements within *all* biblical traditions and texts that perpetuate, in the name of God, violence, alienation, and patriarchal subordination, and eradicate women from historical-theological consciousness. At the same time . . . [we] must recover *all* those elements within biblical texts and traditions that articulate the liberating experiences and visions of the people of God."[29] She likens this work to "the restoration of an old painting which has been painted over again and again."[30] The ethically responsible interpreter, preacher, or reader in pews recognizes that biblical texts are not telling us who God *really* is but are telling us what *biblical writers were saying about God* based on their own ancient experiences from a long time ago in a culture and place quite distinct from our own.

The Bible and the most ancient elements of our Christian tradition reflect the values, cultures, ideologies, morals, and theologies of people from a different era. As such, they are not set-in-stone-for-all-time prescriptions about *what to believe* or *how to be* but instead what *ancient writers believed* and *thought* in antiquity—in Roman Palestine, Asia Minor, Rome, Antioch, Babylon, the southern kingdom of Judah, and so on. Consequently, we do a disservice to Scripture if we try to connect in a one-to-one manner its words with our own time—biblical writers were not speaking to us but to specific audiences in antiquity. The Bible, the Christian tradition, and its robust history of biblical interpretation should be handled today gently and with caution. The Bible and Christian tradition recount *what ancient people said* about God, morals, and religious practice, *not* what any of these things *actually are.*

---

29. Schüssler Fiorenza, 32–33.
30. Schüssler Fiorenza, 164.

Recognizing this distinction is indispensable to a healthy and progressive Christianity. It transforms the phrase "what the Bible says" into an ethical exhortation to "use the Bible responsibly." It converts interpretation into proclamation. Instead of mining Scripture and Christian tradition to discover who God is, we wield both to ask, Which God do you proclaim today— a God of liberation or a God of oppression and violence? It realizes that interpretation is not about extracting truth from Scripture as if the Bible were the final word on every topic but about proclaiming the truth today with the Bible and our sacred tradition as starting points, as springboards for discussing and debating theology, ethics, and politics, even if starting with the Bible and tradition leads to disagreeing with the Bible and tradition. The Bible is not a repository of truth but a repository of ancient human experiences of what is true and sacred.

I sometimes liken the Bible to an uncurated museum filled with paintings (i.e., books) that we might not have included had we been privy to the ancient discussions about the books considered authoritative to establish church doctrine.[31] Had I been around when ancient lists of canonical texts were being written, I would have made a forceful case to include the Gospel of Thomas as a fifth gospel in the New Testament. None of us alive today were part of those ancient discussions, and so, since we did not curate the museum we have inherited, we must meet the challenge as progressive Bible readers to identify and proclaim within this museum "*all* those [truthful] elements . . . that articulate the liberating experiences and visions of the people of God," to borrow again from Schüssler Fiorenza.

---

31. For a survey of canon lists, see Edmon L. Gallagher and John D. Meade, *The Biblical Canon Lists from Early Christianity: Texts and Analysis* (New York: Oxford University Press, 2017).

This is sacred work. It is important work. But work it is. And it starts, I believe, with isolating a fundamental aspect of what it means to be human: relationship. Relationship is the lens through which I read the entire Bible: God's relationship to Godself, God's relationship to people, people's relationship to each other, people's relationship to the planet, Christianity's relationship to Judaism and to other religious traditions, and the relationship of society's privileged to society's underprivileged.

BUBBLES, GOD, AND RELATIONSHIP

Peter Sloterdijk begins his monumental three-volume magnum opus *Spheres* with a story about blowing bubbles to illustrate the centrality of relationship to the human experience:

> The child stands enraptured on the balcony, holding its new present and watching the soap bubbles float into the sky as it blows them out of the little loop in front of his mouth. Now a swarm of bubbles erupts upward, as chaotically vivacious as a throw of shimmer blue marbles. Then, at a subsequent attempt, a large oval balloon, filled with timid life, quivers off the loop and floats down to the street, carried along by the breeze. It is followed by the hopes of the delighted child, floating out into the space in its own magic bubble as if, for a few seconds its fate depended on that of the nervous entity. When the bubble finally bursts after a trembling, drawn-out flight, the soap bubble artist on the balcony emits a sound that is at once a sigh and a cheer. For the duration of the bubble's life the blower was outside himself, as if the little orb's survival depended on remaining encased in an attention that floated out with it. . . . The game continues

tirelessly, once again the orbs float from on high, and once again the blower assists his works of art with attentive joy in their flight through the delicate space. . . . There is solidarity between the soap bubble and its blower that excludes the rest of the world. And each time the shimmering entities drift into the distance, the little artist exits his body on the balcony to be entirely with the objects he has called into existence.[32]

Influenced by Nietzsche and the death of God, Sloterdijk illustrates the ephemeral nature of human existence—it bursts like a soap bubble in the end ("it still had to vanish into nothingness").[33] But he moves beyond Nietzsche's death of God and its bursting bubbles to focus on the bubbles themselves, using this act of creation—of blowing bubbles—to illustrate the fundamental nature of human connection, what he refers to as augmented existence: the bubble blower is in solidarity with his bubbles. Sloterdijk introduces a stunning array of examples of such solidarity from the worlds of art history, philosophy, psychoanalysis, archaeology, Christian history and theology, other religious traditions, literature, science, the classics, and even gynecology. Of the latter, Sloterdijk notes that "no one comes into the world unaccompanied or unattached."[34] We enter this world not alone but connected. We are all connected to our mothers in the womb; and in the womb itself, there is a primal human experience of connection between fetus ("Also") and placenta ("With"). The "With," he says, is "like a nourishing shadow and anonymous sibling": "It is like a dark little

---

32. Sloterdijk, *Spheres*, 1:17–18.
33. Sloterdijk, 1:17.
34. Sloterdijk, 1:413.

brother placed by our side so that the fetal night would not be too lonely; a little sister who, at first glance, is merely there to sleep in the same room with us. One could think its only mission is to share its peace with yours. Like an intrauterine butler, it stays close and on the fringe, discreet and nourishing, privy to our two-party secret, which no one except you and it will ever know about."[35] Sloterdijk's interest in life inside the womb reminds me of Ian McEwan's novel *Nutshell*, told from the perspective of a healthy, full-term fetus that is connected to the outside world through the voices he can hear, the movements of his mother, the podcasts she listens to, the wine she drinks, the food she eats, and the emotions she feels. Sloterdijk sees womb connection as an example of solidarity, what he defines as "the power to belong together."[36] The womb is our primal sphere; "being-in-spheres," he writes, "constitutes the basic relationship . . . , the original product of human coexistence."[37]

Sloterdijk opens up new possibilities for thinking theologically even though borrowing his ideas for theological ends is a bit of a transgression, since he begins with the Nietzschean premise that the God bubble has burst (God is dead). Nevertheless, his theory of spheres is compelling because it helps shed some light on the messiness of God in the Bible. Readers of Scripture encounter a bewildering number of images, names, and actions of God. In the Psalms, God is depicted as a peaceful shepherd, as one who makes wars cease, and also as a conquering warrior and king. God is the source of protection, a rock, a hiding place, a fortress, and a shade. But God is also one who

---

35. Sloterdijk, 1:356–57.
36. Sloterdijk, 1:44.
37. Sloterdijk, 1:45–46.

leads the poets to despair of God's protection when they ask, How long will suffering last? (e.g., Ps 13:2). The Psalms contain songs that approve of ritual processionals to the temple in God's presence and also scorn Israel's burnt offerings. These images do not fit neatly together if one is searching for consistency, but they do make sense if one reads them as songs about relationship. This is not the language of explanation—describing *who God is*—but of how *ancient writers experience* God in relationship.

As almost anyone in a long-term relationship can attest, relationships are messy. They can be filled with ups and downs, with occasional bouts of darkness and shadows broken by periods of rich intimacy, elation, and joy. We fight with our significant others, extended family members, and children, and our children fight with each other. We feud and we make up. We hug, forgive, heal, adjust, and make more room in our lives for others. Relationships are tortuous. They stretch us. But they are also life-giving—built and sustained by our constant decision to love. Such a blending of emotions, of highs and lows, of challenges and transitions, of dark sadness and gleaming beauty *is* what it means to be in a relationship with another person (and with other people). This is why church communities can be so vibrant: we *choose* to love each other in spite of our many differences, in spite of the constant friction engendered by our close proximity to each other.

BUBBLES AND THE BIBLE

It is also why the Bible portrays God in so many sometimes contradictory ways: loving and hating, gracious and unsettling, gentle and explosive, a destroyer and a creator, a stable rock of refuge and an elusive mystery. Consider for example the opening chapters of Isaiah. God's first words in the book speak of a fractured relationship. Isaiah portrays God as a prosecuting attorney who accuses the people of Israel of being rebellious children (Isa 1:2). God calls the city of Jerusalem a "whore" (Isa 1:21) and issues a stunning insult to Israel's leadership by calling them "rulers of Sodom" (Isa 1:10)—a reference to the forsaken cities of Sodom and Gomorrah in Genesis. Roaring through the prophet, God accuses Israel's rulers of being predatory because they "grin[d] the face of the poor" (Isa 3:15). And God despises the people's religious practices of offerings and festivals when the national sins of injustice, oppression, and economic hardship for the least and the lost are daily tolerated (Isa 1:10–17). The prophet scans the moral landscape and sees desolation (Isa 1:7–8).

But the angry voice of the prosecutor is not the only one pouring forth from the prophet. Interspersed throughout the opening chapters of Isaiah are dramatic shifts in tone. Isaiah portrays God's softer side, inviting the people to rebuild the relationship (Isa 1:18–20), accept forgiveness ("though your sins are like scarlet, they shall be like snow"; Isa 1:18; cf. 4:4), and then live into a series of lavish promises. These promises are some of Scripture's grandest: blessings for all nations (Isa 2:2b–3), unending peace that transforms weapons of war into implements of agriculture (Isa 2:4b), and a return to an exodus-like day when God's presence will again dwell powerfully with people as a cloud and a flaming fire (Isa 4:5). This startling tonal transformation resembles the unexpected shifts in "Master's Apprentices" by the metal band Opeth—a song about life, death, and departed friends that breaks up the heaviest of sounds one can find in metal music with gorgeous instrumental riffs: anger and joy, ugliness and beauty, sadness and elation, struggle and freedom. The language of relationship.

The opening chapters of Isaiah are the prophet's words and songs, spoken and sung *as if they were* the very words of God. The depictions of God are the prophet's depictions. The rage is the prophet's rage. The promises are the prophet's own dreams for the people. We readers of Isaiah cannot know whether any of this language originates with God. We also cannot know the degree to which the prophet's words accurately represent the thing called God. But we can say with confidence that these words articulate the prophet's own emotions and describe the prophet's own experience of the divine in the panoply of human emotions from rage to the joy of future hope.

The question for us to wrestle with as we read Isaiah (and as we read Scripture more broadly) is not "What does this text say about God?" (as if the text corresponded in a one-to-one manner with the thing called God). Rather, the question for us to ask ourselves is more nuanced: "How is the writer of this text articulating their experience of God?" Is it blissful, violent, hopeful, peaceful, comforting, terrifying? And more personally, is this my experience of God right now on my own journey of faith? Why or why not? These latter questions pinpoint the relational aspect of Scripture and of people's individual encounters with the sacred, transforming Scripture for us from a statement *about* God into a devotional *encounter with* the sacred source of life.

This liberates us to be honest with our emotions around the concept of God. We might be baffled at God like the suffering Job. We might haltingly accept God's promises like fickle Abraham. We might scoff at God's promises like laughing Sarah. We might struggle with God like limping Jacob. We might even despair of God's presence like crucified Jesus. We can also be confident in God like Saint Paul or question God like the psalmists. We can be honest about experiencing God as absent or ineffectual like the writer of Ecclesiastes.

All of this language is the language of spheres, the language of relationship. Scripture is a repository of human experiences of the divine: doubting, trusting, raging, despairing, laughing, loving. It is the language of relationship *with* and *within* God. This is why we progressive Christians can be so open and accepting of difference and of different theological persuasions (or the absence of theological persuasion). We recognize that all God-talk, from passionate to despairing, from raging to hoping, *is* the language of relationship with God. It is why, ontologically speaking, there is no such thing as a death of God—God's death is simply one experience among many that people have *of* God; the death of God says nothing about God as such. But it is also why we can fully embrace our rich heritage as Christians, including its most orthodox manifestations. God incarnated in human flesh in the person of Christ is quintessentially relational—a God who dwells among us and is discovered in the faces of the people we meet (see Matt 25:35–40). God as Spirit (or Wind, or Breath) is fully present with us, breathing life into and through our communities and our personal interactions. And God as triune implies that God is an eternal, intraloving relationship.

BUBBLES AND TRINITARIAN COMMUNITY

Peter Sloterdijk ends the first volume of the *Spheres* trilogy by discussing the trinity and, more specifically, the Greek concept from the seventh-century church that Father John of Damascus called *perichoresis*: the interaction of the three persons (Father, Son, and Holy Spirit) *within* the triune God:

> Perichoresis means that the milieu of the persons is entirely the relationship itself. The persons contained in one another in the shared space locate themselves in such a way that they illuminate and pervade and surround one another, without being harmed by the clarity of their difference. One could say that they are as invisible as air to one another ... each one inhales and exhales what the others are—the perfect conspiration; each breaks forth from Himself into the others—the perfect protuberance. They provide neighborhood for one another—the perfect being-surrounded.
>
> The characteristic of living together or in one another . . . does not belong to the intra-godly persons [alone], but also manifests itself, in a sense, in human associations of persons. . . . At its medieval zenith, Trinitarian theology . . . led . . . to the discovery of a language for the *strong relationship*.[38]

I recognize again that using the Nietzschean Sloterdijk to reassert the God concept is transgressive; however, the language of relationship here is profound. It draws out a fundamental aspect of what it means to be human: in, with, and through community, we experience that which is most sacred to us. Or to put this differently, in, with, and through community, we experience the God who *is* community. Isaiah's experience of God was precipitated by Isaiah's (angry) encounter with the community of Israel. Saint Paul speaks of God in the context of early Christian communities called churches. Job's encounter

---

38. Sloterdijk, 1:607, 614 (italics original).

with God is in the presence of his community of friends. Even Jesus on the cross quotes from Psalm 22, a song meant for communal worship.

God is experienced in community, in interacting with and relating to others. God calls to us, writes poet Christian Wiman, "in the everyday voices of other people."[39] The Psalms are again instructive here because they are filled with personal language—"the Lord is *my* shepherd" (Ps 23:1; italics mine)—that almost always has a liturgical function in the context of a worshipping community. Speaking, praying, singing, and chanting the Psalms are ways for the faithful to remind each other of their collective relationship with God. The centrality of relationship also helps fill out the elementary theological statement in the New Testament Letter of First John: "God is love" (1 John 4:7). The word *love* in Greek is not just a noun—it is also a verb: "to love." It is a decision, not a feeling, and it implies that there is *another* whom one chooses to love. If God *is* love, then God as triune in our tradition is a way of saying that God is a plurality of persons loving one another—a love that ripples outward and suffuses our own relationships, which are modeled on divine love. God is encountered in the midst of our human interactions and in the midst of our loving; we literally meet God in the faces of strangers and friends. This is why passing of the peace in a Sunday-morning worship service is so liturgically and theologically important. Passing the peace of Christ is not just a moment in the service to stretch our legs, greet our friends, and welcome visitors; it is also theology in action—encountering God in another and transforming the fundamental human experience of relationship into something divine. Refocusing God-talk around the Sloterdijkean concept

---

39. Wiman, *My Bright Abyss*, 122.

of spheres or relationships frees us up to think differently about the concept of God and about how God relates to us.

Take one example from the M. Night Shyamalan film *Signs*. In a scene that takes place on a living room couch, the protagonist Graham, an ex-priest who lost his faith after his wife was tragically killed in a car crash, is sitting beside his younger brother, Merrill. Graham and Merrill are watching live news footage of alien ships that have entered Earth's atmosphere and positioned themselves strategically around the world. The two brothers are discussing whether this is the end. Graham explains to his younger brother that there are two possible responses to the presence of aliens, represented in the views of two different kinds of people. One group of people looks at the alien ships and thinks this could be the end of the world. Since people in this group believe that there are no coincidences in life, they trust that Something—perhaps it is God—is ultimately in control, and this brings them comfort. The other group looks at the alien ships and thinks their presence could be either good or bad, but whatever happens, people in this group believe that they are ultimately on their own, and this fills them with fear. So, says Graham, each of us has to ask ourselves which kind of person we are: Do we believe that there are no coincidences? At this point in the film, Graham believes we are all on our own, but his perspective changes after a series of unlikely events comes together to save the lives of his children and brother—events that seem like more than mere coincidence. He even reenters the priesthood at the end of the film. It is a powerful story, but one with a giant theological hole in the plot: If there are no coincidences, then what do we make of the tragic death of Graham's wife? The film never answers this question. We the viewers are left to draw the disturbing conclusion that even her death was purposed. What purpose did it serve exactly? To lead her husband out of and then back into the priesthood?

Some people will try to prove the existence of God by pointing to events in their lives that seem like more than coincidence. Their stories can be emotionally gripping, and they may be signs that Something bigger than ourselves is at work. But these are dangerous theological waters to enter because the questions begin to multiply. Rabbi Brad Hirschfield dealt with this after 9/11. People were thanking God that they escaped the burning buildings, using the language of *divine plan* or *God's will* to justify their good fortune. Hirschfield highlighted the flip side of such theology:

> You want plan? Then tell me about plan. But if you're going to tell me about how [God's] plan saved you, you'd better also be able to explain how the plan killed them. And the test of that has nothing to do with saying it in your synagogue or your church. The test of that has to do with going and saying it to the person who just buried someone and look in their eyes and tell them, "God's plan was to blow your loved one apart." Look at them and tell them that God's plan was that their children should go to bed every night for the rest of their lives without a parent. If you can say that, well, at least you're honest. I don't worship the same God.[40]

As a minister, I have spent enough time with the bereaved to know intimately how seductive the craving can be for answers to life's tragedies. I also know that any answers we might think we have discovered are fleeting—a temporary theological sugar

---

40. "Faith and Doubt at Ground Zero," *Frontline*, PBS, September 3, 2002, https://tinyurl.com/y4w4knkt.

rush. Focusing on events that seem like more than coincidence to prove God's existence or to bolster our faith is to enter the theological trap set by the film *Signs*; it is to enter a world of unanswerable questions or questions with disturbing answers. I think a better approach focuses on the relationship between Graham and Merrill. Their interaction on the couch *is where God is found.* And our connection to the people who lived and died on 9/11—our empathy for them and the terror they endured—*is* where God is found. God is discovered in human interaction: in our relationships with each other, in our spheres. Christian Wiman has written beautifully of our connection to each other: "It is not some meditative communion with God that I crave. What one wants during extreme crisis is not connection with God, but connection with other people; not supernatural love, but human love. No, that is not quite right. What one craves is supernatural love, but one finds it only within human love. This is why I am, such as I am, a Christian, because I can feel God only through physical existence, can feel his love only in the love of other people."[41]

The God we should proclaim from pulpits and from the pages of Scripture is a relational God—a God who entered human flesh to commune with us, a God in Spirit who moves through us in our communities of faith, a God who the prophets say wants us to care for the poor and the disenfranchised because being poor and disenfranchised is a failure of relationship in society and working for justice in society is a way to repair this fractured relationship. Our connection to each other, to our planet, to those who suffer, and to those who advance humanity through invention and ingenuity *is* where God is found. We see God in the faces of others—their beauty,

---

41. Wiman, *My Bright Abyss*, 163–64.

diversity, pain, struggles, and simple acts of kindness. We encounter God's love in *our* loving. Fifth-century theologian Pelagius once said that God is present in all things:

> Look at the animals roaming the forest: God's spirit dwells within them. Look at the birds flying across the sky: God's spirit dwells within them. Look at the tiny insects crawling in the grass: God's spirit dwells within them. Look at the fish in the river and sea: God's spirit dwells within them. There is no creature on earth in whom God is absent. . . . Look too at the great trees of the forest; look at the wild flowers and the grass in the fields; look even at your crops. God's spirit is present within all plants as well. The presence of God's spirit in all living things is what makes them beautiful; and if we look with God's eyes, nothing on earth is ugly.[42]

Pelagius's words make me think of a comment by Yoda the Jedi Master in the film *Empire Strikes Back*: "Feel [God] around you. Between you and me, the tree, the rock, everywhere."[43] Moving through us. Surrounding us. Binding us together. Breathing in and through our very breath. Discovered and experienced in our connections with each other and with our planet. The word *God* is the word we use to describe this sense of connection.

---

42. J. Philip Newell, *Listening for the Heartbeat of God: A Celtic Spirituality* (London: SPCK, 1997), 10–11.

43. Irvin Kershner, dir., *The Empire Strikes Back* (San Francisco: Lucasfilm, 1980), DVD.

3
PICTURES OF JESUS

Christ is always being remade in the image of man [sic], which means that his reality is always being deformed to fit human needs, or what humans perceive to be their needs. A deeper truth, though, one that scripture suggests when it speaks of the eternal Word being made specific flesh, is that there is no permutation of humanity in which Christ is not present. If every Bible is lost, if every church crumbles to dust, if the last believer in the last prayer opens her eyes and lets it all finally go, Christ will appear on this earth as calmly and casually as he appeared to the disciples walking to Emmaus after his death, who did not recognize this man to whom they had pledged their very lives; this man whom they had seen beaten, crucified, abandoned by God; this man who, after walking the dusty road with them, after sharing an ordinary meal and discussing the scriptures, had to vanish once more in order to make them see.

—Christian Wiman, *My Bright Abyss*

The New Testament gospels depict Jesus Christ in a series of pictures. Each one crafts or fashions its own truth. The 2016 film *Their Finest* illustrates the process. The film tells the story of screenwriters Tom Buckley and Catrin Cole. While working together on the script of a British propaganda film about the rescue of British soldiers at Dunkirk during World War II, they discover, to their dismay, that the rescue story that had provided the plot for their film was historically untrue. Buckley saves the film, however, when he announces that the historicity of the plot doesn't matter because, he says, "we pick our truths."[1] Philosopher Friedrich Nietzsche once suggested something similar when he observed that philosophy is a form of autobiography, that what counts as "truth" is intimately connected to an individual's personal story—their experiences, upbringing, tastes, preferences, and sense of identity. In *Beyond Good and Evil*, Nietzsche writes, "It has gradually become clear to me what every great philosophy up till now has consisted of— namely, the confession of its originator, and a species of involuntary and unconscious autobiography."[2] Like Nietzsche, Buckley recognizes that "we pick our truths" based on what resonates with us—based on the stories we are trying to tell each other or tell ourselves. Buckley insists that the propaganda film's narrow focus on a boat piloted by twin sisters who ferry British soldiers to safety represents a thousand other stories of tiny fishing boats employed in the service of rescue. The film's story is "true," he argues, because it represents bigger truths.

THE GOSPELS AS DISTINCT WORKS OF ART

The New Testament gospels reflect these same insights. The gospels do not all tell the same story about Jesus. Each gospel,

---

1. Lone Scherfig, dir., *Their Finest* (2016; London: BBC Films, 2017), theater.

2. Friedrich Nietzsche, *Beyond Good and Evil: Prelude to a Philosophy of the Future*, trans. Helen Zimmern (Stilwell, KS: Digireads, 2005), 9.

like a distinct work of art, possesses its own distinctive features and its own distinctive truth. Each is its own picture, to borrow a concept from the Cure's "Pictures of You." Mark is not quite like Matthew or Luke; Matthew is different from Luke; John's story is not the same as that of Mark, Matthew, or Luke.

Consider a few examples. In John's Gospel, Jesus's ministry lasted for three years, while in Matthew, Mark, and Luke, it was just one. We know this based on the number of times Jesus visited Jerusalem to celebrate Passover (three times in John and only once in the other gospels). Many such discrepancies exist among the four gospels. Was Jesus crucified on the day the Passover lamb was sacrificed (John)? On the day after (Matthew, Mark, and Luke)? What were Jesus's final moments on the cross like? Did he die fully in control, willingly giving himself over to death (Luke and John)? Or despairing and anguished with the words of Psalm 22:1 on his lips, "My God, my God, why have you forsaken me" (Mark and Matthew)? The gospels differ on the number of angels that were beside or inside the empty tomb on Easter. They tell different stories about whether the disciple Peter had a chance to see the empty tomb for himself, whether he met the risen Jesus, and whether the risen Jesus appeared to his disciples at all (Mark's Gospel ends abruptly without any postresurrection appearance stories). The gospels disagree over whether the Jewish law in the first five books of the Bible is still binding for followers of Jesus. They disagree over what Jesus said when he spoke in parables or whether he even spoke in parables (John's Gospel lacks parables). They do not all contain the same stories about Jesus's miracles. And only two of them (Matthew and Luke) contain what is arguably the most well-known teaching of Jesus from the Sermon on the Mount, which contains the material about loving enemies and turning the other cheek, even though the two versions disagree on the content of the sermon as well as on the place where Jesus delivered it (Matthew puts Jesus on a mountain; Luke puts him on a level place). Moreover, the four gospels each begin their stories differently. Matthew and Luke have Christmas stories; Mark and John do not. The Christmas stories in Matthew and Luke do not agree on the details: Luke has shepherds, angels, a Roman census, a manger, and baby Jesus wrapped in swaddling clothes; Matthew has a series of dreams, murderous King Herod, and the wise men following a star in the east. (Read the first two chapters of the Gospels of Matthew and Luke before putting up your nativity scene near the Christmas tree next year. nativity scenes conflate the two stories.)

Few casual readers, regular churchgoers, or dedicated lay readers of the gospels notice these discrepancies. And many evangelical clergy and scholars who are aware of these discrepancies, and ought to know better, try to shrug them off by saying that they somehow complement each other—this was how my seminary professors tried to explain away the discrepancies and how I used to explain them away to myself. But the differences among the gospels are significant. Each tells its own story.

EXCURSUS: JESUS'S BAPTISM

Take the example of Jesus's baptism, which is recounted with different details in each of the four New Testament gospels. Mark's version is the most straightforward, stating that Jesus "was baptized by John in the Jordan [river]" (Mark 1:9). Matthew's version adds more detail—John resists baptizing Jesus when he says, "I need to be baptized by you, and do you come to me?" (Matt 3:14). Jesus then convinces John that his baptism is necessary, and John concedes. Luke's version of this story removes John completely. Luke 3:19–20 mentions that John was in prison for criticizing King Herod and his wife, Herodias. The very next story in Luke's Gospel is the baptism of Jesus, and it never says who it was that did the baptizing (Luke 3:21–22). Most surprising of all is that Jesus never actually gets baptized in John's Gospel (John 1:29–34). No one knows for sure why it is that these stories differ so drastically, but one possibility is that the Gospels of Matthew, Luke, and John struggled with the meaning of baptism as it relates to Jesus. If baptism is a symbolic washing away of sins, then why would a sinless Jesus need to be baptized? Matthew solves this problem by portraying Jesus as insisting that he needs to be baptized. Luke (sort of) solves this problem by removing John the Baptist from the story and discretely stating that Jesus got baptized (Luke's version could be interpreted to mean that Jesus baptized himself). And John solves this problem by not having Jesus get baptized at all. The point is that the gospel writers can and do sometimes differ when they tell the stories of Jesus.

EXCURSUS: JESUS, FOOD, AND HAND WASHING

Another interesting difference among the gospels is in how they address the issue of Jewish kosher food (i.e., food from the Jewish legal tradition that Jews do not eat—e.g., pork). New Testament scholarship has a long tradition of recognizing that each gospel writer used sources when compiling their gospels. The gospel writers were more like editors who cut and paste than like authors writing from scratch. The majority of scholars, including many evangelical scholars, hold that Matthew and Luke had independent access to the Gospel of Mark and to another lost gospel called the "Sayings Source," or "Q" (from the German word *quelle*, which means "source"). Q is a gospel composed almost entirely of Jesus's words—no healing stories, no passion narrative, no Christmas or Easter stories. Just Jesus the talking head. John's Gospel is independent of this Mark-Q stream of sources, which helps explain why John is so different in many ways from the other three gospels. If Matthew and Luke both used Mark as a source, then those places where they do different things with Mark's Gospel or where they disagree with Mark are illuminating. How these three gospels treat kosher food is one such example.

You can see in the following examples how Matthew and Mark address this issue in one of the so-called controversy stories where Jesus argues with other religious leaders. Interestingly, Luke omits the story altogether. There are several minor differences between Mark's version and Matthew's version. The more significant differences are underlined:

Mark 7:1–23	Matthew 15:1–20
1 Now when the Pharisees and some of the scribes who had come from Jerusalem gathered around him, 2 they noticed that some of his disciples were eating with defiled hands, that is, without washing them. 3 (For the Pharisees, and all the Jews, do not eat unless they thoroughly wash their hands, thus observing the tradition of the elders; 4 and they do not eat anything from the market unless they wash it; and there are also many other traditions that they observe,	1 Then Pharisees and scribes came to Jesus from Jerusalem and said, 2 "Why do your disciples break the tradition of the elders? For they do not wash their hands before they eat." 3 He answered them, "And why do you break the commandment of God for the sake of your tradition? 4 For God said, 'Honor your father and your mother,' and, 'Whoever speaks evil of father or mother must surely die.' 5 But you say that whoever tells father or mother,

the washing of cups, pots, and bronze kettles.) **5** So the Pharisees and the scribes asked him, "Why do your disciples not live according to the tradition of the elders, but eat with defiled hands?" **6** He said to them, "Isaiah prophesied rightly about you hypocrites, as it is written,

> 'This people honors me with their lips, but their hearts are far from me; **7** in vain do they worship me, teaching human precepts as doctrines.'

8 You abandon the commandment of God and hold to human tradition." **9** Then he said to them, "You have a fine way of rejecting the commandment of God in order to keep your tradition! **10** For Moses said, 'Honor your father and your mother'; and, 'Whoever speaks evil of father or mother must surely die.' **11** But you say that if anyone tells father or mother, 'Whatever support you might have had from me is Corban' (that is, an offering to God)—**12** then you no longer permit doing anything for a father or mother, **13** thus making void the word of God through your tradition that you have handed on. And you do many things like this."
14 Then he called the crowd again and said to them, "Listen to me, all of you, and understand: **15** there is nothing outside a person that by going in can defile, but the things that come out are what defile."
[v. 16 is lacking in some ancient manuscripts.]

'Whatever support you might have had from me is given to God,' then that person need not honor the father. **6** So, for the sake of your tradition, you make void the word of God. **7** You hypocrites! Isaiah prophesied rightly about you when he said:

> **8** 'This people honors me with their lips, but their hearts are far from me; **9** in vain do they worship me, teaching human precepts as doctrines.'"

10 Then he called the crowd to him and said to them, "Listen and understand: **11** it is not what goes into the mouth that defiles a person, but it is what comes out of the mouth that defiles." **12** Then the disciples approached and said to him, "Do you know that the Pharisees took offense when they heard what you said?" **13** He answered, "Every plant that my heavenly Father has not planted will be uprooted. **14** Let them alone; they are blind guides of the blind. And if one blind person guides another, both will fall into a pit." **15** But Peter said to him, "Explain this parable to us." **16** Then he said, "Are you also still without understanding? **17** Do you not see that whatever goes into the mouth enters the stomach, and goes out into the sewer? **18** But what comes out of the mouth proceeds from the heart, and this is what defiles. **19** For out of the heart come evil intentions, murder, adultery, fornication, theft, false witness, slander.

17 When he had left the crowd and entered the house, his disciples asked him about the parable. **18** He said to them, "Then do you also fail to understand? <u>Do you not see that whatever goes into a person from outside cannot defile,</u> **19** <u>since it enters, not the heart but the stomach, and goes out into the sewer?"</u> (Thus he declared all foods clean.) **20** And he said, "It is what comes out of a person that defiles. **21** For it is from within, from the human heart, that evil intentions come: fornication, theft, murder, **22** adultery, avarice, wickedness, deceit, licentiousness, envy, slander, pride, folly. **23** All these evil things come from within, and they defile a person."	**20** These are what defile a person, but to eat with unwashed hands does not defile."

Note: This story is not in Luke's Gospel.

Notice that there are several minor differences between the two versions of this story. Both gospels quote from Isaiah 29:13 but do so in different places in the dialogue. Mark places the quotation in verses 6–7, before Jesus accuses the religious leaders of breaking the commandment in favor of their tradition, while Matthew places it after Jesus makes this accusation. In Mark's version, Jesus enters a house where the disciples ask him to explain his teaching. In Matthew's version, there is no house and it is only Peter who asks for an explanation. In Matthew, the disciples inform Jesus that he had offended the Pharisees, and Jesus accuses the Pharisees of being blind guides. Neither of these details appears in Mark's version. There is also a small host of differences at the level of grammar and wording—keeping in mind that these stories were originally written in Greek, not English.

There are at least two ways to explain why this story doesn't appear in Luke. One possible explanation is that Luke was writing his gospel for gentile readers with little knowledge of Jewish tradition, for whom arcane debates between Jesus and other religious leaders over Jewish legal tradition, especially food laws, would have seemed irrelevant. Or put differently, Luke's audience (the first readers or hearers—ancient texts were often read aloud to audiences) probably comprised people who ate pork and who would have assumed that Jesus had no problem with them doing so. A discussion about kosher food for these early Christians would have been irrelevant, so Luke omits the story completely.

A second possible explanation goes to the heart of Luke's own literary agenda. Luke is careful to portray Jesus throughout his gospel as being faithful to Jewish tradition. Fidelity to one's ancestral heritage was a cherished value in the ancient Greco-Roman world. At the beginning of Luke's Gospel, for example, an infant Jesus is circumcised on the eighth day in accordance with the law of Moses (Luke 2:21). When Jesus is twelve, Luke presents him as engaging in a theological discussion with Jewish religious leaders who were amazed at his knowledge of the tradition (Luke 2:46–47). Luke even adds a comment that Jesus's parents, Mary and Joseph, had "performed everything according to the Law of the Lord"—that is, the law of Moses (Luke 2:39 ESV). Luke presents an adult Jesus as beginning his public ministry not by calling disciples but by entering a synagogue "as was his custom" to preach (Luke 4:16). Luke's Jesus is a faithful Jew, adhering closely to his centuries-old tradition. Conversely, Mark's Jesus breaks decisively with this tradition in the story about hand washing and kosher food.[3] Mark adds,

---

3. There is some debate among New Testament scholars over whether Mark's Gospel does actually break with Jewish tradition. I am following the majority perspective here, but James G. Crossley, "Halakah and Mark 7:3: 'With the Hand in the Shape of a Fist,'" *New Testament Studies* 58, no. 1 (2012): 57–68, makes a forceful argument to the contrary.

"Thus [Jesus] declared all foods clean," a statement that effectively nullifies Jewish kosher laws (Mark 7:19). Even though Mark was one of Luke's sources, Luke deliberately chose not to include this story in his version possibly because Mark, in Luke's mind, had gone too far in presenting Jesus as breaking with his ancestral tradition. Luke's painting or picture of Jesus is different from that of Mark's.

Matthew chose to include this story from Mark's Gospel about hand washing and kosher food but made a few significant changes. Here are the underlined differences in side-by-side columns:

Mark 7:3–4, 11, 18–19	Matthew 15:5, 20
3 (For the Pharisees, and all the Jews, do not eat unless they thoroughly wash their hands, thus observing the tradition of the elders; 4 and they do not eat anything from the market unless they wash it; and there are also many other traditions that they observe, the washing of cups, pots, and bronze kettles.) 11 "Whatever support you might have had from me is Corban" (that is, an offering to God) 18 "Do you not see that whatever goes into a person from outside cannot defile," 19 (Thus he declared all foods clean.)	5 "Whatever support you might have had from me is given to God" 20 but to eat with unwashed hands does not defile

Notice that Matthew lacks Mark's explanatory comments about hand washing (Mark 7:3–4) and changes Mark's wording about offerings to God (Mark 7:11 and Matt 15:5). Matthew also lacks the explanatory comments in Mark 7:18–19 about Jesus declaring all foods (even nonkosher foods) clean.

As with Luke's decision to omit this story altogether from his gospel, these differences may be attributed to differences in audience—different readers or hearers. Mark may have been writing to an ethnically mixed audience of Jews and gentiles, the latter of whom needed some explanation of arcane Jewish religious practices. So Mark placed some explanatory comments onto the lips of Jesus about hand washing (vv. 3–4) and added the Aramaic word *Corban* to explain to his readers (or hearers) what Jewish offerings were called (v. 11). When I say "put onto the lips of Jesus," I mean that literally. I doubt that Jesus spoke in the exact way that Mark portrays him as speaking in this story; Mark is crafting Jesus for his audience. Matthew's audience, on the other hand, may have been primarily or even completely composed of ethnic Jews, who would not have needed such explanations. So Matthew omits them and crafts a different image.

GOSPEL WRITERS AS ARTISTS

The gospel writers, like any preacher in a pulpit today, shaped and edited the words of Jesus—shaped the message of the gospel itself—to speak to the needs of their audiences. And Matthew goes further than just making minor adjustments to Mark's Jesus. By omitting the explanatory comment from Mark's Gospel about Jesus declaring all foods clean (Mark 7:19), Matthew is disagreeing with Mark's presentation of the teaching of Jesus. In Mark's version, a dispute between Jesus and the religious leaders over hand washing has been transmuted into a broader message about Jesus declaring all foods (even nonkosher foods) clean. In effect, Mark presents Jesus as nullifying centuries of Jewish and biblical tradition about kosher food. Such a dramatic expansion of Jesus's words was probably unacceptable to Matthew and his ethnically Jewish audience, most of whom would have kept Jewish law; so Matthew stays focused on the primary issue of hand washing, portraying Jesus as majoring on majors and minoring on minors, which is why Matthew's Jesus returns to the issue of hand washing at the end of the story, saying, "To eat with unwashed hands does not defile" (Matt 15:20). Matthew's Jesus doesn't overthrow Jewish tradition and biblical law; instead, his Jesus preserves such major traditions while downplaying the more minor traditions about religious hand washing.

The point is that Matthew and Mark are not saying the same things. They are not saying complementary things. They simply disagree. Each writer has painted a different picture of Jesus. One is of a Jesus who is broadening the horizon of what is considered religiously acceptable by declaring all foods clean and overthrowing accepted religious norms (Mark). The other presents Jesus as still very much within the established and centuries-old tradition of his forebears with only slight modifications (Matthew). These are not the same messages, yet both are contained in Scripture.

CELEBRATING CONTRADICTIONS

As a progressive Christian, discrepancies and even outright contradictions in the Bible are not problems to be solved or threats to one's faith but rather differences to be celebrated. These contradictions enhance the power of the New Testament gospels by making them more diverse and colorful. Such diversity reinforces for me that people encounter Jesus (and God, as we saw in the last chapter) in different ways and that each person's journey of faith, including the journeys of faith of biblical writers, is unique to them. No two people encounter Jesus (or God) in the same way, which means that the gospels reflect the gospel writers' own perspectives of Jesus. Each creative presentation of Jesus is like a distinct painting. Added to these four New Testament accounts are more than thirty other noncanonical gospels in early Christianity, several of which are useful to scholars today as they try to reconstruct the life and times of the historical figure of Jesus. But each gospel, whether it is part of the New Testament or not, is its own work of art. Gospel writers pick and shape their truths, to borrow again from Tom Buckley, and they write (or paint) under the influence of their own autobiography, to borrow again from Nietzsche.

Progressive Christians commonly say that they follow the example of Jesus or pay close attention to the teachings of Jesus when they talk about what it means to be a Christian. The late New Testament scholar and committed Christian Marcus Borg famously said that if the Bible and Jesus disagree, "Jesus wins."[4] Although this quip has a catchy bumper sticker–like quality, the irony, as Borg himself admitted, is that we read about the example of Jesus in the gospels of this very same Bible. And not only do these gospels not present Jesus in the same way; they also do not reproduce in a straightforward manner the words and deeds of the actual, historical Jesus who walked the earth two thousand years ago. The gospels are presentations of Jesus written decades after he died and *thus reflect the values and interests of the writers and editors who compiled them.*

---

4. Marcus J. Borg, *The Heart of Christianity: Rediscovering a Life of Faith* (San Francisco: HarperSanFrancisco, 2003), 81.

THE HISTORICAL PROBLEM OF JESUS

Scholars of the gospels have been forced to admit this fact even though they disagree over whether it's possible to sift the various gospels to identify the bits and pieces that go back to the historical Jesus himself. Some scholars are quite confident that the application of rigorous methods will yield something close to the actual, historical Jesus. Other scholars (I include myself in this latter group) are skeptical. One reason we are skeptical is that the various scholarly reconstructions of the life and times of the historical Jesus differ so drastically from each other that it strains credulity to believe they are all talking about the same guy. While this reason by itself is not sufficient to deny the possibility of accessing the historical Jesus (after all, perhaps scholars haven't yet found the right methodological key to unlock the historical Jesus door), it does suggest that there is a problem with trying to reconstruct the life and times of Jesus. Some scholars say Jesus was an apocalyptic prophet, others that he was a revolutionary peasant, others that he was an ethical sage, still others that he was a Jewish magician, and others still that Jesus was an Aryan (yes, "Aryan," as some Nazi scholars argued in the 1930s)—the list goes on and on. The most recent popularized reconstruction of the historical Jesus was that of Reza Aslan's in *Zealot: The Life and Times of Jesus of Nazareth*.[5] Aslan's book was published at the tail end of several centuries of scholarly searching for the historical Jesus with little to show for it except more reconstructions and more books with no two being exactly the same. In fact, many of these books simply recycle and repackage the ideas of previous scholars with slight

---

5. Reza Aslan, *Zealot: The Life and Times of Jesus of Nazareth* (New York: Random House, 2013).

modifications. Aslan's book falls into this category, which is why scholars familiar with the centuries-long quest for the historical Jesus greeted it with a wide yawn.

Scholar Francis Watson, who has written a fine summary of gospel literature even though his general approach and conclusions have been (rightly, in my view) criticized by other specialists, has argued that the gospels are each a "distinctive perspective" on Jesus; each one, he says, is a "portrait of Jesus" that fills out the truth of what Jesus means like a good "metaphor can communicate truth." Watson goes further: "There is no access to the singular, uninterpreted reality of a 'historical Jesus.'"[6] Each gospel, he says, "is nothing less than a new interpretation of the figure of Jesus, qualitatively different from its precursor. . . . [This] assumes that earlier gospel writing is not definitive, and that the traditions it embodies need to be articulated again in the light of new interpretative insights."[7]

William Arnal, another expert in gospel literature, goes even further than Watson. He argues in a Nietzschean fashion that scholarly reconstruction of the historical Jesus is akin to autobiography: scholars peer into the well of history when trying to describe the historical Jesus and see their own reflections peering back, which they then describe as if it were the actual, historical figure of Jesus.[8] Arnal concludes,

Perhaps the quest for the historical Jesus should be abandoned. . . . Not because scholars cannot agree on their reconstructions; lack of agreement may only indicate that

---

6. Francis Watson, *Gospel Writing: A Canonical Perspective* (Grand Rapids, MI: Eerdmans, 2013), 605–6.

7. Watson, 286.

8. This observation was first made by George Tyrrell, *Christianity at the Crossroads* (London: Longman, Green, 1910).

further—and more rigorous—work needs to be done. Not because the investigation has been biased; bias is unavoidable, here as elsewhere. Not even because reasonable conclusions are impossible in light of our defective sources, though this may indeed be the case. But because, ultimately, the *historical* Jesus does not matter, either for our understanding of the past, or our understanding of the present. . . . The Jesus who is important to our own day is not the Jesus of history, but the symbolic Jesus of contemporary discourse.[9]

To state the matter plainly, the Jesus who matters is not the Jesus we think we can reconstruct from the sources of the ancient past but rather the Jesus we proclaim today using the pages of Scripture as our starting point. On those pages, we encounter diverse presentations of Jesus. Each ancient gospel—like each modern-day sermon—is a new proclamation of Jesus for a new audience in a different time and place from Jesus's own.

The Gospel of Mark portrays Jesus as a divine man (or human being) for a majority gentile audience for whom the abilities to heal, raise the dead, and cast out demons were known traits among divinely inspired wonder-workers in the ancient Greco-Roman world. Apollonius of Tyana, for example, was a known wonder-worker in the first century, and he, like Jesus, raised the dead, healed the sick, and had disciples.

The Gospel of Matthew differs from Mark in that it closely connects the wonder-working Jesus to Jewish tradition, possibly because Matthew was writing to ethnic Jews who were followers of Jesus. Matthew's Jesus says that each little piece of

---

9. William Arnal, *The Symbolic Jesus: Historical Scholarship, Judaism and the Construction of Contemporary Identity*, Religion in Culture (London: Equinox, 2005), 77.

Jewish law down to its minutest punctuation marks is still valid (Matt 5:17–20).

The Gospel of Luke is different from Matthew and Mark. It presents Jesus with the attributes of a Greco-Roman benefactor who dispenses good things to others (a lauded trait in the ancient world), which would have appealed to an educated gentile audience. Luke's Jesus is noted for his piety when he hangs out in the temple as a child (Luke 2:49), he piously prays at every significant moment of his life, he is known for his good or frank speech (Luke 4:22; 24:19), and he shows clemency toward his enemies when he forgives those who crucified him (Luke 23:34)—all traits of the good person in antiquity.[10]

The Gospel of John is different still, depicting Jesus as a more divisive figure particularly with respect to his relationship with his fellow Jews. John also presents those who are sympathetic to the message of Jesus as being an embattled and persecuted group of followers. John may be reflecting the increasing divisions between Jews and the followers of Jesus in his own day when he writes about those who confess Jesus as the Messiah being put out of the synagogue (John 9:22).

JESUS FOR TODAY

Each gospel writer took the traditions and stories about Jesus and reworked them for an audience living in a new day and time. This same process continues today. Elisabeth Schüssler Fiorenza portrays Jesus as proclaiming "an alternative world free of hunger, poverty, and domination." His movement, she says, was about "inclusive table-sharing," "healing and liberating

---

10. I owe all of these insights to my PhD thesis advisor, John Kloppenborg.

practices," and "domination-free kinship." And it "found many followers among the poor, the despised, the ill and possessed, the outcasts, prostitutes, and sinners."[11] Schüssler Fiorenza's presentation of Jesus speaks powerfully to today's poor, oppressed, and marginalized.

Artist Timothy Schmalz, reflecting modern Catholic social teaching, has depicted Jesus as a homeless man shrouded in a blanket that covers his face and sleeping on a park bench.[12] The viewer knows that it is Jesus because his bare feet peek out from beneath the blanket, and both feet have nail-pierced scars. The image is unforgettable. I remember the day I first saw this image. I was approaching the entrance to the Regis College Library at the University of Toronto when I noticed a man sleeping on a park bench just to the left of the front door. As I got closer, I realized that it was a bronze sculpture of a full-grown man, and I saw his nail-pierced feet. It evoked for me all those places in the gospels where Jesus identifies completely with the poorest and the most vulnerable.

Each presentation of Jesus, whether it's a sculpture, a painting, or a painting with words on a page, is, to borrow again from William Arnal, a Jesus who matters for us today. The issue to keep in mind when reading the gospels, he says, "is not whether or how the events recounted in the gospel stories intersect with actual historical events; rather, the issue is the overall effect of the story itself on attitudes and conceptions of the self and others."[13] The question for today, in other words, is what effect do

---

11. All quotes come from Schüssler Fiorenza, *Jesus and Politics of Interpretation*, 170.

12. Timothy P. Schmalz, "Homeless Jesus," Sculpture by Timothy P. Schmalz, accessed February 26, 2021, https://tinyurl.com/y3pxzd9x.

13. Arnal, *Symbolic Jesus*, 52.

the stories of Jesus have on us? In what ways is the colorful and diverse Jesus from the past speaking today?

Diverse paintings of Jesus in the New Testament gospels invite us to think more critically and creatively about how he might still be speaking. In my denomination, the United Church of Christ (UCC), we use the phrase "God is still speaking," but such a phrase could just as easily be modified to "Jesus is still speaking." In the dispute between Jesus and the religious leaders over kosher food and hand washing, I see in the contradictory presentations of Jesus in Matthew and Mark at least two important truths. Sometimes we need to hear about the importance of honoring religious traditions while always keeping in mind that God cares about our hearts and longs for us to major on the majors and minor on the minors. This is *a* message from Matthew among many others that could be preached. From Mark, we might glean the insight that religious traditions can sometimes stifle and smother. When they are at their worst, such traditions become so routine and rigid that fidelity to them ends up mattering more than showing compassion to fellow human beings. And so, in moments like these, we need the Jesus of Mark to remind us of the importance of breaking free from traditions that can become dehumanizing—we need to hear that all foods are clean, so to speak—so we can explore fresher ways to *be* progressive people of faith today. This is *a* truth from Mark's sacred text among many others that could be preached.

Each presentation of Jesus in the gospels is distinctive, offering a Jesus who speaks differently depending on what we might need him to say. Sometimes it is a Markan Jesus who speaks to us; other times it is a Matthean or a Lukan or a Johannine Jesus. Sometimes the gospels don't speak as clearly to us, and so we might turn to innovative presentations of Jesus in art, songs, poems, or films. Denys Arcand's 1989 film *Jesus of*

Montreal offers a modern depiction of Jesus. The film is about a Passion play that angers church authorities and transforms the protagonist (Daniel) into a kind of Jesus figure who sacrifices his life but then lives on in a new theater company started by his friends.

Scholars, artists, screenwriters, songwriters, gospel writers, street protesters, poets, preachers, the list goes on and on—each one gives Jesus a new voice. But each is a voice that is solidly grounded in tradition. The gospel writers creatively borrowed, edited, updated, and reworked the first-century traditions about Jesus's words and deeds. We also creatively borrow, edit, update, and rework those same gospels that are grounded in tradition to make Jesus speak to us today. Progressive Christianity stands firmly on centuries of tradition—a tradition that is, as is the Bible we read, a *place to start.*

TWO STORIES FROM THE GOSPELS

Let me end this chapter with two more examples of how we might update the gospels for today. The first is from a story that appears in different places in the Gospels of Matthew, Mark, and Luke (but not at all in John) about the healing of a man with leprosy.[14] I have always preferred Mark's version of this story, perhaps because of the gentle, human touch that Mark adds to

---

14. "Leprosy" was not modern-day Hansen's disease. See the discussion of leprosy and of this story in particular in Matthew Thiessen, *Jesus and the Forces of Death: The Gospels' Portrayal of Ritual Impurity within First-Century Judaism* (Grand Rapids, MI: Baker, 2020), ch. 3. Thiessen interprets this story differently than I do here by emphasizing not Jesus's compassion but his anger based on a different rendering of Mark's Greek text.

the narrative. In each version of the story, a man with leprosy approaches Jesus and begs to be healed. Matthew and Mark present the leprous man as kneeling and begging. Luke says he fell on his face before Jesus, pleading. But only in Mark does it say that Jesus was "moved with pity"—that he was filled with compassion. The Greek word means something like "feeling deeply in one's guts." Mark's Jesus aches when he sees the man: "A leper came to him begging him, and kneeling he said to him, 'If you choose, you can make me clean.' Moved with pity, Jesus stretched out his hand and touched him, and said to him, 'I do choose. Be made clean!' Immediately the leprosy left him, and he was made clean" (Mark 1:40–42). Casual readers might fixate on the cleansing part and miss the miracle that precedes it. There are two miracles in this story. One—the physical healing of a skin disease—is the obvious miracle that only Jesus could do. The other miracle practically demands to be replicated today by the followers of Jesus. Mark elongates the language to describe it: "Jesus stretched out his hand and touched him." Mark could have simply said, "Jesus touched the man" or that Jesus said to the man, "Go in peace, your faith has saved you." Instead, Mark expands the language, adding words about Jesus *stretching out his hand*. The miracle here is the touch itself.

People in Jewish antiquity avoided those with leprosy out of fear that they would spread impurity to others. Lepers were regarded as physically unfit to enter the temple compound in Jerusalem until they could prove to a priest that they were clean and thus ritually acceptable. Furthermore, to touch a leper would render the one who did the touching unclean, making them unfit to enter sacred spaces. Philosopher Thomas Nail argues that borders of all sorts, whether fences, barricades, security checkpoints, or temple walls, are not designed to stop the flow of people as much they are designed to control it.[15] Laws around leprosy in ancient Judaism were not created to prevent access to God as much as they were designed to control *who* had such access. Jesus shamelessly traverses this border, this controlling of access, and in so doing, he undoes the power of staid religious tradition that tried to control access to God for outsiders. By touching the leper, Jesus embodies the principle that all people have direct access to God.

This story begs to be applied in our day, when so many of our LGBTQ+ siblings feel barred from entering churches. They aren't lepers but have been made to feel like lepers. And because of the irrational fears of many non-Muslims, our Muslim siblings, too, have been made to feel marginal—a marginality concretized in travel bans and hate crimes. If Jesus was moved with pity—if his guts ached for outsiders—enough to cross a rigid border and perform a touching miracle, surely we, his followers, can touch and even embrace those who have been made to feel marginal in our world.

The second story is the well-known parable of the Good Samaritan, which only appears in Luke's Gospel. Scholars like John Dominic Crossan have argued that even though this story doesn't have multiple attestations, it sounds like something the historical Jesus would have said, and so the story or at least part of it was probably spoken by the actual, historical Jesus. Crossan and others are guessing here, but whether this conjecture is correct is beside the point. The story is in one of our New Testament gospels and is part of our sacred tradition and thus has the power to teach and, even more, to be taken seriously as

---

15. Thomas Nail, *Theory of the Border* (New York: Oxford University Press, 2016).

a place to start when thinking about how to *be* as people of faith today. This famous story goes as follows:

> Just then a lawyer stood up to test Jesus. "Teacher," he said, "what must I do to inherit eternal life?" He said to him, "What is written in the law? What do you read there?" He answered, "You shall love the Lord your God with all your heart, and with all your soul, and with all your strength, and with all your mind; and your neighbor as yourself." And he said to him, "You have given the right answer; do this, and you will live."
>
> But wanting to justify himself, he asked Jesus, "And who is my neighbor?" Jesus replied, "A man was going down from Jerusalem to Jericho, and fell into the hands of robbers, who stripped him, beat him, and went away, leaving him half dead. Now by chance a priest was going down that road; and when he saw him, he passed by on the other side. So likewise a Levite, when he came to the place and saw him, passed by on the other side. But a Samaritan while traveling came near him; and when he saw him, he was moved with pity. He went to him and bandaged his wounds, having poured oil and wine on them. Then he put him on his own animal, brought him to an inn, and took care of him. The next day he took out two denarii, gave them to the innkeeper, and said, 'Take care of him; and when I come back, I will repay you whatever more you spend.' Which of these three, do you think, was a neighbor to the man who fell into the hands of the robbers?" He said, "The one who showed him mercy." Jesus said to him, "Go and do likewise." (Luke 10:25–37)

As with the debate over hand washing and kosher food, the parable begins with a legal discussion. A lawyer puts a question to Jesus about how to gain a place in the age to come, how to be saved in modern evangelical parlance. Rabbi Jesus responds by asking the lawyer what he thinks. The lawyer answers by summarizing the twin pegs of the Jewish law: love God and love the neighbor. Jesus praises his answer and seems ready to end the discussion until the lawyer presses further, wanting clarification: "And who is my neighbor?" Jesus then launches into a story about how a man was traveling on a dangerous road from Jerusalem to Jericho when he was attacked, beaten, robbed, and left for dead. The clergy of the day—the priest and the Levite (an ordained temple worker)—saw the man but passed by on the other side of the road without stopping to help.

Although Jesus as an Aramaic speaker probably did not tell this story in Greek, Luke's Greek version surprises at this point in the story because of how he organizes the wording. Greek word order is flexible in a sentence, and sometimes writers emphasize certain words by placing them at the beginning of sentences. In this story, the next word after we read about the priest and the Levite is *Samaritan*. The word jumps off the page. Our English bibles tend to gloss the punchiness of Luke's Greek by introducing the Samaritan as "But a Samaritan." But Luke's Greek is jarring and could be more literally translated as "likewise also a Levite, having approached the place and seeing [the half-dead man] passed on the other side. Samaritan(!) then approached . . ." Notice the difference between how Luke introduces the Levite and how he introduces the Samaritan— *Samaritan* intrudes. Jesus goes on to describe the wonderful humanitarianism of this Samaritan: he cleaned and bandaged the man's wounds, he lifted the wounded man onto his donkey and transported him to an inn to recover, and he then paid the man's medical bills and promised to pay any additional costs. The Samaritan's compassionate action is beautiful and has inspired generations of people to be Good Samaritans, shoveling snow for homebound folks or stopping to help a stranded traveler whose car has broken down. As in the story about Jesus touching the leper, the Samaritan *ached in his guts* for the half-dead man (Luke uses the same Greek word as Mark to describe this aching), and the compassionate aching led to action.

Samaritans were ethnic and religious "others." They were the descendants of the ancient northern tribes of Israel, who worshipped in a different sacred place (Mount Gerizim) than the temple in Jerusalem, who followed a different liturgical calendar, and who read a different sacred text (the Samaritan Pentateuch). They were considered unorthodox. Put more strongly, Samaritans—from the point of view of the religious majority— were from the wrong religion, were members of the wrong ethnic group, worshipped in the wrong sacred place, read the wrong sacred text, and held the wrong views about religious purity. They were the Muslims of their day, the people with AIDS, the undocumented migrants, the folks in gender transition, the African American males in hoodies, the theological skeptics, the *others*.

Had Luke's Jesus wanted to tell a story about helping someone on the side of the road, he could have simply talked about three different people, one of whom stopped to help. And had Luke's Jesus wanted to irritate the religious establishment of his day, he could have simply made the third person a Jewish layperson or peasant. But the interjection of *Samaritan* in the story sets up a far more striking contrast that goes deeper than just distinguishing between good people who help and bad people who don't and goes deeper than making a dig at the clergy who have more religious things to do than help a wounded human being. This story hacks apart our fetishes with ethnic and religious purity, our "us versus them" paradigms. It is challenging precisely because of how Jesus draws attention to a Samaritan, an "other." This parable, like the story of touching a leper, breaches boundaries and teaches us to critically evaluate all the fences and borders that we erect to control who has access to God. The walls dividing acceptable and unacceptable religion (Christian versus Muslim, Christian versus Jew, etc.), theology (orthodox versus heretic), gender identity (binary versus fluid), race, or class—all human-made walls come crashing down because *Samaritan*. What matters in the story—what matters to Jesus and thus to God—is how one acts toward another person, especially a wounded person, not whether someone has checked all the right theological boxes or fits neatly into a prescribed box called "normal." Again, this is because *Samaritan*.

PICKING OUR TRUTHS

When we pick our truths as we interpret the New Testament gospels, our responsibility as progressive Christians is to privilege those portions of the gospels that depict (or paint) Jesus in ways that are consistent with the boundary-crossing message we find in Mark's story of the touching of the leper and Luke's parable of the Good Samaritan. I think this can be a powerfully compassionate way to read the gospels and then apply them to today.

Each gospel is a compilation of several bits and pieces of stories and sayings of Jesus, and the writers have added their own distinctive veneer—their own distinctive artistic flares—to their works of art. And like good works of art, the importance, significance, and even beauty of the gospels are all completely lost if the diverse imagery is forced into a single mold; the gospel artists didn't all paint the same story except in broad strokes. Their portraits of Jesus invite us into another world—the world as the gospel artists want us to see it. As we gaze at these ancient paintings of Jesus—as we dwell in the worlds the gospel writers construct—things begin to look different in *our* world. *We* change, and the truths we pick may even change. To follow Jesus—to have faith in Jesus—is to take a step into the boundary-crossing worlds the gospel writers construct for us. We will be stretched beyond what is comfortable. But comfortable faith is no faith at all.

4

SAINT PAUL THE PROGRESSIVE

A first line should open up your rib cage. It should reach in and twist your heart backward. It should suggest that the world will never be the same again.

—Colum McCann, *Letters to a Young Writer*

[Paul's] message was that all people, in accordance with their common nature as creatures, should view themselves as members of a single commune created by God. . . . If understood, this news should result in the dissolution of the enmities that arise among individuals and groups.

—Peter Sloterdijk, *God's Zeal*

What we see [in the Bible] depends on where we stand.

—Elisabeth Schüssler Fiorenza, *Rhetoric and Ethic*

THE HUMANITY OF RELIGION

Reading Jonathan Z. Smith revolutionized my understanding of religion as a graduate student. It opened up my rib cage—to borrow wording from writer Colum McCann. Smith was a professor of religion at the University of Chicago, and his writings were the first lines in a new chapter of the academic study of religion—a movement that blended the familiar with the strange in order to defamiliarize his readers with what they thought they knew about religion. He helped me see religion differently. In one stimulating article, Smith transformed my understanding of biblical interpretation by detailing the interpretive practices of Ndembu diviners.[1] Borrowing from the ethnographic work of cultural anthropologists, Smith wrote of the Ndembu,

> The chief mode of Ndembu divination consists of shaking a basket in which some 24 fixed objects are deposited (e.g., a cock's claw, a piece of hoof, a bit of grooved wood, a black withered fruit). These are shaken in order to winnow out "truth from falsehood" in such a way that a few of the objects end up on the top of the heap. These are "read" by the diviner with respect to both their individual meanings and their combinations with other objects and the configurations that result. The client's situation is also taken into account in arriving at an interpretation. . . . The total collection of 24 objects is held to be complete and capable of illuminating every situation.

Smith goes on:

> What enables the fixed canon of divinatory objects in the diviner's basket to be applied to every possible situation or

---

1. Jonathan Z. Smith, "Sacred Persistence: Toward a Redescription of Canon," in *Imagining Religion: From Babylon to Jonestown* (Chicago: University of Chicago Press, 1982), 50–51.

question is not the number of objects . . . nor the breadth of their range of meanings. Rather it is that, prior to performing the divination, the diviner has rigorously questioned his client in order to determine the latter's situation with precision. The diviner functions with respect to his client much as the successful preacher functions with respect to his [*sic*] congregation. Application, here, is not a generalized systematic process, but a homiletic endeavor, a quite specific attempt to make the "text" speak to a quite particular situation.

Smith pinpoints a key aspect of weekly preaching: connecting a sacred text drawn from a canon of sacred writings to the specific needs of a congregation. Applying portions of a fixed canon to the needs of a particular audience by an authoritative interpreter is familiar to churchgoers. Smith discovered this same process at work in settings outside of institutional churches among the Ndembu. By showing how other cultures follow this same pattern with their own sacred canon (bits of hoof, wood, and withered fruit instead of a Bible) and their own sacred interpreters (diviners instead of preachers), Smith reveals how human the whole process of interpreting sacred texts (written or not) is: an authorized interpreter examines the sacred text and applies it to the lives of others. Hermeneutics and homiletics are thus shown to be human projects, not merely Christian ones.

Smith's insight is consistent with the anthropological (i.e., human/social) dimension of religion, a cornerstone of the study of religion for the past century and a half. Religion has power in part because of its capacity to bind humans together in community even as it also helps them make sense of their world. The legendary scholar of religion Émile Durkheim attempted to probe beneath religious symbols to isolate their social realities, arguing that "religion is an eminently social thing."[2] Even "the most bizarre or barbarous [religious] rites and the strangest myths," he wrote, "translate some human need and some aspect of life, whether social or individual."[3] Smith adds to Durkheim's analysis the insight that religion is a "mode of constructing worlds of meaning." It creates space, he says, "in which to meaningfully dwell."[4] Religion helps us make sense of our world. It makes meaning and builds community. Scholars who research this human and social side of religion have helped us recognize that many Christian religious practices are not unique to Christians. Ndembu diviners are a case in point.

PAUL THE INTERPRETER AND THE INTERPRETERS' PAUL

These sociological insights shed light on the letters of Saint Paul in the New Testament. Like Ndembu diviners, Paul was an interpreter of sacred tradition. He interpreted sacred texts and traditions and applied those interpretations to the lives of early Christians in the congregations that he founded. In so doing, he not only carved out for his readers a distinct identity "in Christ" (one of Paul's favorite phrases); he also created a space in which they could meaningfully dwell. He established

---

2. Émile Durkheim, *The Elementary Forms of Religious Life*, trans. Karen E. Fields (New York: Free Press, 1995), 9.

3. Durkheim, 2.

4. Jonathan Z. Smith, "Map Is Not Territory," in *Map Is Not Territory: Studies in the History of Religions* (Chicago: University of Chicago Press, 1993), 290–91.

social communities (i.e., churches) and gave the people in those communities a sense of meaning and a shared identity. This is important to keep in mind as we read Paul's letters because we are in effect reading someone else's mail. Paul did not write to us today. He established communities and then created meaning and constructed identity in each of his letters for specific people at a specific time in the first century CE. We, by contrast, enter the world of Paul's letters after centuries of interpreters have picked over his words, forced him into theological boxes, and most disturbingly of all, weaponized his writings (and the New Testament letters written in his name) to do battle with those deemed to be heretics, with Jews, with LGBTQ+ people, and with anyone else deemed to be "other." Paul's letters have been a carcass, and many of his interpreters have been the vultures.

The letters of Paul have been used in Christian history to fight the abolition of slavery, to argue that women shouldn't preach in churches, to keep LGBTQ+ folks closeted, and (among many other things) to support racist and oppressive political policies in the name of abiding by the rule of law. US Attorney General Jeff Sessions quoted Romans 13 during a press conference in June 2018 to justify the Trump administration's zero-tolerance policy of prosecuting every person, both child and adult, who crosses the southern border without documentation. The relevant section of Romans 13 reads as follows:

> Let every person be subject to the governing authorities; for there is no authority except from God, and those authorities that exist have been instituted by God. Therefore whoever resists authority resists what God has appointed, and those who resist will incur judgment. For rulers are not a terror to good conduct, but to bad. Do you wish to have no fear of the

authority? Then do what is good, and you will receive its approval; for it is God's servant for your good. But if you do what is wrong, you should be afraid, for the authority does not bear the sword in vain! It is the servant of God to execute wrath on the wrongdoer. (Rom 13:1–4)

Sessions said, "I would cite to you the Apostle Paul and his clear and wise command in Romans 13, to obey the laws of the government because God has ordained the government for his purposes." He went on to say, "Orderly and lawful processes are good in themselves. Consistent and fair application of the law is in itself a good and moral thing, and that protects the weak, it protects the lawful."[5] After this press conference, *Washington Post* reporters Julie Zauzmer and Keith McMillan dug into American history to locate other times when Romans 13 was cited. Their research led them to John Fea, professor of American history at Messiah College (my alma mater). Fea noted that "there are two dominant places in American history when Romans 13 is invoked. One is during the American Revolution [when] it was invoked by loyalists, those who opposed the American Revolution. The other is in the 1840s and 1850s, when Romans 13 was invoked by defenders of the South or defenders of slavery to ward off abolitionists who believed that slavery is wrong. I mean, this [argument that Sessions makes] is the same argument that Southern slaveholders and the advocates of a Southern way of life made."[6]

---

5. Julia Jacobs, "Sessions's Use of Bible Passage to Defend Immigration Policy Draws Fire," *New York Times*, June 15, 2018, https://tinyurl.com/ybx9r9qy.

6. Julie Zauzmer and Keith McMillan, "Sessions Cites Bible Passage Used to Defend Slavery in Defense of Separating Immigrant Families," *Washington Post*, June 15, 2018, https://tinyurl.com/uxxj4cl.

Vultures picking over the Romans 13 carcass used this ancient text to oppose the American Revolution and to support the institution of slavery. While few in the US today would deny that the American Revolution was justified and that slavery was morally wrong, many eighteenth- and nineteenth-century Christians did, and they used these verses in Paul's letters to buttress views with divine authority.

In the early days of the civil rights movement, white clergy in Alabama published an op-ed in local newspapers on April 12, 1963, which reinforced an earlier statement they had made that year titled "An Appeal for Law and Order and Common Sense." Their op-ed stated that "racial matters [should] properly be pursued in the courts" and, further, that decisions of the courts should "be peacefully obeyed." They went on to call the "demonstrations" against segregation in Birmingham "unwise and untimely."[7] Dr. Martin Luther King Jr. was jailed during these protests, wrote "Letter from Birmingham Jail" from his cell in response to these white clerics, and made the case that their appeal to law and order was immoral. King argued that the Birmingham legal system, its mayors and courts, was not color-blind but rather was inclined to preserve the segregation status quo. As King noted, "Privileged groups seldom give up their privileges voluntarily" and "freedom is never voluntarily given by the oppressor."[8] The call of white clergy to wait for a timelier moment, wrote Dr. King, "rings in the ear of every Negro with piercing familiarity. This 'Wait' has almost always meant 'Never.'" Freedom, said Dr. King, "must be demanded by the oppressed." But on what theological grounds could one

---

7. "Statement by Alabama Clergy," Stanford University, April 12, 1963, https://tinyurl.com/y7d54kks.

8. King, "Letter from Birmingham Jail."

engage in civil disobedience and break the law after Saint Paul's declaration in Romans 13:1–2 that the "governing authorities . . . have been instituted by God" and that "whoever resists authority resists what God has appointed"? King responded,

> There are two types of laws: just and unjust. I would be the first to advocate obeying just laws. One has not only a legal but a moral responsibility to obey just laws. Conversely, one has a moral responsibility to disobey unjust laws. I would agree with St. Augustine that "an unjust law is no law at all."
>
> Now, what is the difference between the two? How does one determine whether a law is just or unjust? A just law is a man made code that squares with the moral law or the law of God. An unjust law is a code that is out of harmony with the moral law. To put it in the terms of St. Thomas Aquinas: An unjust law is a human law that is not rooted in eternal law and natural law. Any law that uplifts human personality [i.e., human well-being] is just. Any law that degrades human personality is unjust. All segregation statutes are unjust because segregation distorts the soul and damages the personality.[9]

Some human laws (such as the segregation laws of the Jim Crow South) are so out of touch with the way God intends human societies to function that they *must* be broken. Obeying unjust laws is morally wrong.

King's response to the southern white clergy is consistent with a long tradition of civil disobedience in Christian history. In the early second century CE, Pliny the Younger, the Roman governor of Bithynia, wrote to the emperor Trajan for guidance on how to deal with Christians who remained intransigent when

---

9. King.

pressed by the governing authorities to recant their beliefs. The Pliny-Trajan correspondence marks a key moment in Christian history because it provides evidence that the Roman governing authorities were beginning to realize that Christians were their own religious group with practices and beliefs that were different from those of their Jewish siblings in faith. Jews were familiar to the Romans, but Christians were new, and Romans were skeptical of novelty. So, Pliny writes to Trajan,

> I was never present at any trial of Christians; therefore I do not know what are the customary penalties or investigations, and what limits are observed. . . . This is the course that I have adopted in the case of those brought before me as Christians. I ask them if they are Christians. If they admit it I repeat the question a second and a third time, threatening capital punishment; if they persist I sentence them to death. For I do not doubt that, whatever kind of crime it may be to which they have confessed, their pertinacity and inflexible obstinacy should certainly be punished. . . . Thereupon the usual result followed; the very fact of my dealing with the question led to a wider spread of the charge, and a great variety of cases were brought before me. . . . All who denied that they were or had been Christians I considered should be discharged, because they called upon the gods at my dictation and did reverence, with incense and wine, to your image which I had ordered to be brought forward for this purpose, together with the statues of the deities; and especially because they cursed Christ, a thing which, it is said, genuine Christians cannot be induced to do. . . . I thought it the more necessary . . . to find out what truth there was in this by applying torture to two maidservants, who were called deaconesses. But I found nothing but a depraved

and extravagant superstition, and I therefore postponed my
examination and had recourse to you for consultation. . . .
The contagion of this superstition has spread not only
in the cities, but in the villages and rural districts as well; yet
it seems capable of being checked and set right.[10]

Trajan replied to Pliny with words of encouragement: "You
have taken the right line, my dear Pliny, in examining the cases
of those denounced to you as Christians, for no hard and fast
rule can be laid down, of universal application. They are not
to be sought out; if they are informed against, and the charge
is proved, they are to be punished."[11] Christians in the early
second century were being hauled before a Roman governor
to be examined, and some of them refused to obey the laws
and customs of the Romans. These laws and customs obligated
residents of the empire to prove their patriotism by calling on
the Roman gods and by honoring the image of the emperor.
Ancient Jews were exempted from these laws and customs
because of the antiquity of their religion. Romans permit-
ted them to pray and offer sacrifices *on behalf of* the emperor
rather than *to* the emperor. But Christians weren't afforded the
same exemption.[12] Pliny's letter indicates that Christians were
tortured and executed for their disobedience.

For the next two hundred years, Christians were periodi-
cally judged to be enemies of the Roman state. Christian tradition has often remembered its earliest centuries as an age of
persecution in which the Romans continuously targeted the

---

10. Quoted in Henry Bettenson and Chris Maunder, eds., *Documents of
the Christian Church* (New York: Oxford University Press, 2011), 3–4.

11. Bettenson and Maunder, 5.

12. See Bruce W. Winter, *Divine Honours for the Caesars: The First Christians' Responses* (Grand Rapids, MI: Eerdmans, 2015), 110.

followers of Christ. But, as scholar Candida Moss has argued, persecution of Christians was at most sporadic during this time period (though it did occur).[13] In the mid-second century, for example, a Christian leader in Smyrna named Polycarp was executed for refusing to swear allegiance to the emperor. The Roman proconsul demanded that Polycarp renounce Christianity by cursing Christ. Polycarp is purported to have replied, "We [Christians] are taught to render to authorities and the powers ordained of God [only] the honor that is fitting"—that is, not to accord them divine honors. Hearing this, bystanders accused Polycarp and other Christian teachers of being "destroyer[s] of our gods." Polycarp was then sent to the flames. Near the end of the second century, Christians in Lyons and Vienne were subjected to appalling persecution at the hands of local mobs and magistrates. One Christian leader named Plotinus was interrogated by the governor, who asked the old saint to describe the Christian God. "If you are worthy, you shall know," Plotinus responded.[14] He was then pummeled mercilessly by onlookers for his obstinance. During the reigns of emperors Valerian (mid-third century) and Diocletian (early fourth century), the property of Christians was seized, churches were razed to the ground, Scriptures were destroyed, and demands were made that the followers of Christ honor the gods and the emperor. Persecution in each of these instances was a Roman response to the steadfast resistance by Christians to follow what they believed were the idolatrous and immoral laws and customs of the state.

---

13. Candida Moss, *The Myth of Persecution: How Early Christians Invented a Story of Martyrdom* (New York: HarperOne, 2013).

14. Quoted in Bettenson and Maunder, *Documents of the Christian Church*, 9–14.

Many other Christians have been persecuted for similar acts of civil disobedience in the ancient world and in times closer to our own. Martin Luther put his life on the line and sparked the Protestant Reformation with his "here I stand, I can do no other" moment of resistance to Catholic doctrine that demanded unflinching loyalty to the pope. Abolitionist Christians risked prison and heavy fines for disobeying the Fugitive Slave Act of 1850 by participating in the Underground Railroad. German theologian Dietrich Bonhoeffer was involved in the resistance to Hitler's Nazi government and its anti-Semitic and racist laws. Bonhoeffer was eventually arrested and executed. And, of course, Saint Paul himself was accused of "turning the [Roman] world upside down" in his ministry (Acts 17:6). Paul finished his career writing letters from a Roman prison before his own execution at the hands of the state. All of these examples could be seen as footnotes to the example of Jesus Christ. Crucifixion was first and foremost a tool of imperialism and a political sentence deployed against enemies of the Roman Empire.

When Dr. King justified civil disobedience to governing authorities by appealing to the ideal law of God (the eternal law) that "uplifts human personality," he carried on a long tradition of Christian resistance to immoral governing authorities. "Letter from Birmingham Jail" outlines a certain posture Christians ought to have in the societies in which they live: laws and customs that "degrade human personality"—laws and customs that denigrate human beings, who are created in God's image—should be transgressed, while laws and customs that "uplift human personality" are to be obeyed because they are consistent with God's will for human society.[15] Incidentally, Dr. King's

---

15. King, "Letter from Birmingham Jail."

insights render completely ridiculous the claims made by many conservative evangelicals today that they are being persecuted because their freedom of speech or freedom of religion is under attack when they, for example, refuse to bake wedding cakes, prepare flower arrangements, or make wedding invitations for gay couples.[16] It's the refusal to provide such services that degrades human personality, not vice versa.

There is an analogy to be drawn between Dr. King's "eternal law" that "uplifts human personality" and the interpretation of Scripture. As with human laws, so with the human interpretation of Scripture, *any interpretation that degrades human personality (i.e., human well-being) should be rejected in favor of interpretations that uplift human personality.*

This is a crucial insight for progressive Christians. Rather than wielding the Bible as a club to beat and bully, we commit to wielding it as a tool to build and uplift. It's *a place to start* as we discover new ways to be more compassionate in our world and compassionate toward our fellow human beings and toward our precious planet. In her 2009 TED talk, scholar Karen Armstrong talked about the centrality of compassion in the world's religious traditions:

> For years I've been feeling frustrated, because as a religious historian, I've become acutely aware of the centrality of compassion in all the major world faiths. Every single one of them has evolved their own version of what's been called the Golden Rule. Sometimes it comes in a positive version— "Always treat all others as you'd like to be treated yourself."

---

16. See the summary in Laura M. Holson, "How Battles over Same-Sex Couples Play Out in Court," *New York Times*, July 17, 2019, https://tinyurl.com/y3yo4wav.

And equally important is the negative version—"Don't do to others what you would not like them to do to you." Look into your own heart, discover what it is that gives you pain and then refuse, under any circumstance whatsoever, to inflict that pain on anybody else. . . .

But you know you'd never know it a lot of the time, that this was so central to the religious life. Because with a few wonderful exceptions, very often when religious people come together, religious leaders come together, they're arguing about abstruse doctrines or uttering a council of hatred or inveighing against homosexuality or something of that sort. Often people don't really want to be compassionate. I sometimes see when I'm speaking to a congregation of religious people a sort of mutinous expression crossing their faces because people often want to be right instead.[17]

Armstrong has labored to change people's "mutinous expression[s]."[18] She helped found the Charter for Compassion, which is committed to making the world a better, more compassionate place. The charter says we can do this by recognizing that "compassion impels us to work tirelessly to alleviate the suffering of our fellow creatures, to dethrone ourselves from the center of our world and put another there, and to honor the inviolable sanctity of every single human being, treating everybody, without exception, with absolute justice, equity, and respect."

Of particular relevance when interpreting Saint Paul's letters is what the charter says about interpretations of Scripture:

---

17. Karen Armstrong, "Let's Revive the Golden Rule," filmed July 2009 in Oxford, UK, TED video, 9:54, https://tinyurl.com/y5mlk6us.

18. Armstrong.

"Any interpretation of scripture that breeds violence, hatred, or disdain is illegitimate."[19]

Almost from its beginning, Christian history has valued Paul's letters (and the New Testament letters written in his name) as Scripture. Paul's words, like the objects in Ndembu diviner baskets, continue to be interpreted and applied to the lives of people millennia after he wrote them. Today they are put to use in contexts he could never have imagined. (I write this in the spirit of irony as I work on a lecture titled "Paul the Master of Social Media.") Interpreting Paul's writings—like trying to identify the actual historical Jesus as we saw in the previous chapter—is like peering into a mirror: we see a bit of ourselves and our values in these ancient texts. So if someone reads Paul's letters and comes away affirming the institution of slavery, the oppression of women, the condemnation of LGBTQ+ people, or the hatred of immigrants—interpretations that lack compassion and degrade the human personality—then we should not only reject such interpretations, but we should also ask ourselves what is wrong with such interpreters, *not* what is wrong with Paul. To be sure, parts of Paul's letters have raised some ethical red flags for Christians through the ages—Paul was a man of his (ancient) time—but he wasn't writing to us, which means that when we read his letters, we are interpreting for our own time, following the same process as Ndembu diviners. How we interpret Paul—how we weaponize him in our debates—says more about us than it does about Paul.

One would need to know something about the twisted world of Trump's America to understand why Attorney General

---

19. "The Charter for Compassion," Charter for Compassion, accessed February 26, 2021, https://charterforcompassion.org/charter/affirm.

Jeff Sessions could quote Paul as an authority to justify the administration's mistreatment of immigrants. The same is true when we examine the appalling history of anti-Semitism in Christian history, much of it fueled by weaponizing Paul. Martin Luther wielded Paul's letters to write abhorrent things about Jews in a treatise titled *On the Jews and Their Lies*.[20] Luther accused the Jews of crucifying and blaspheming Christ, he labeled them miserable and accursed, he said their theology was filled with venom and rancor, and he called their religious practices poisonous. Undergirding all of Luther's animosity was his interpretation of Paul's letters, which, he claimed, drove a wedge between law and gospel. The law was Jewish and pointed to sin; the gospel was Christian and pointed to freedom and salvation. Thus in Luther's mind, Jews who continued to reject the gospel in favor of the law were serving the devil. Instead of interrogating Paul when we read Luther's words, we should be interrogating Luther himself: What was wrong with Luther that made it possible for *him* to proclaim such hate against Jews in the name of Paul? When Sessions and Luther appeal to Paul to support their hate-filled views, it says more about *them* than it does about Paul because, as interpreters, they are selecting from Paul's letters those bits and pieces that they wish to use to justify their hate.

SEEING AND STANDING

Hermeneutics and ethics are intertwined. Do we read and interpret the Bible in order to be right or in order to be more

---

20. See William R. Russell, ed., *Martin Luther's Basic Theological Writings* (Minneapolis: Fortress, 2012), ch. 46.

compassionate? No one approaches Scripture as a purely neutral or objective reader. We don't read Paul's letters *and then* develop our ethics. The interpretations we draw out of Paul's letters are *already* shaped by our ethical grids, and these ethical grids are themselves shaped by our life situations. To put this another way, *what we see depends on where we stand.*

In an article examining African American approaches to biblical interpretation, Demetrius K. Williams provides an example of this principle of interpretation by quoting a fascinating exchange in 1833 between a white Presbyterian plantation missionary named Charles Colcock Jones and a congregation of enslaved Black people.[21] The quotation is drawn from Jones's memoir:

> I was preaching to a large congregation on [Paul's] Epistle to Philemon: and when I insisted upon fidelity and obedience as Christian virtues in servants and upon the authority of Paul, condemned the practice of [enslaved people] running away, one half of my audience deliberately rose up and walked off with themselves, and those that remained looked anything but satisfied, either with the preacher or his doctrine. After dismission, there was no small stir among them; some solemnly declared "that there was no such an Epistle in the Bible"; others, "that they did not care if they ever heard me preach again." . . . There were some too, who had strong objections against me as a Preacher, because I was a master.[22]

---

21. Demetrius K. Williams, "African American Approaches: Rehumanizing the Reader against Racism and Reading through Experience," in *Studying Paul's Letters: Contemporary Perspectives and Methods,* ed. Joseph A. Marchal (Minneapolis: Fortress, 2012), 164.

22. Demetrius, 164.

This exchange illustrates that enslaved African Americans and a white antiabolitionist preacher were interpreting Paul's Letter to Philemon through grids shaped by their different life experiences. Charles Colcock Jones simply assumed that God willed the institution of slavery, and he wielded Paul's writings to support his assumption. But "enslaved African Americans," writes Williams, "*were not* convinced that it was God's will for them to be slaves, no matter what the Bible, their 'masters,' or pro-slavery preachers and exegesis told them," and some of them were content to dismiss Jones outright and never listen to him preach again.[23] Life situations shape ethical and moral grids, and these grids influence our hermeneutics. North American interpreters in a capitalist context interpret the politics in Paul's letters differently than Latin American interpreters do in more socialist ones. African American Christians in urban contexts read Paul's use of the exodus story in his letters differently than white evangelicals do in the suburbs. Nigerian Christians in a postcolonial context read Paul's statements about spiritual gifts differently than British Christians do in London. The list goes on and on. *What we see* in the Bible *depends on where we stand.* Elisabeth Schüssler Fiorenza argues that "context is as important as text. What we see depends on where we stand. One's social location or rhetorical context is decisive for how one sees the world, constructs reality, or interprets biblical texts."[24]

This statement implicates *every* interpreter: Jeff Sessions and Martin Luther, abolitionists and antiabolitionists, enslaved African Americans and white southern masters, modern American evangelicals and mainline Christians, churchgoers in the

---

23. Demetrius, 165.

24. Schüssler Fiorenza, *Rhetoric and Ethic*, 19.

pews and preachers who deliver the word on Sundays. *Every* interpreter, even Paul himself. After all, he too was an interpreter of the sacred tradition embedded in the Hebrew Scriptures and in the story of Christ's death and resurrection. Paul was by no means a neutral interpreter of this tradition; his own social location shaped the language and thought-forms he used in his letters.

PAUL THE PERSON, PAUL THE WRITER

We learn a good deal about Paul's complicated identity from his letters. And when I say "letters," I'm referring specifically to those letters that are unanimously attributed to Paul by New Testament scholars, the so-called authentic letters: Romans, First and Second Corinthians, Galatians, Philippians, First Thessalonians, and Philemon. The six other New Testament letters that claim Pauline authorship are "disputed"—Ephesians, Colossians, Second Thessalonians, First and Second Timothy, and Titus. "Disputed" means it is not certain that Paul himself wrote them. The language, theology, moral guidelines, and more formalized ecclesiastical offices in these letters seem to reflect a later stage of development in Christian history after Paul's death. The practice of writing under a pseudonym (in this case, "Paul") was fairly common in the ancient world, so it is possible that one or many of Paul's disciples wrote letters in his name sometime later in the first century or early in the second century. The writers of Second Thessalonians admit that such a phenomenon was occurring when they refer to messages "by word or by letter, as though from us" (2 Thess 2:2b). There are also a few noncanonical Christian texts that claim a connection to Paul, such as the Acts of Paul and Thecla and the Apocalypse of Paul. Writing in Paul's name was a bit of a cottage industry in early Christianity.

By focusing on the authentic letters, we can read Paul in his own words before later writers began layering on interpretations shaped by their own experiences and social locations. The authentic letters contain various statements that provide some information about Paul's identity. We learn from these letters that Paul was a male Greek-speaking Jew and Pharisee, educated, conversant in Roman political discourse, able to navigate gentile and Jewish settings, and utterly convinced that he had experienced a miraculous and personal encounter with the risen Christ that transformed his worldview.

Paul writes about his earlier life in Judaism: "I advanced in Judaism beyond many among my people of the same age, for I was far more zealous for the traditions of my ancestors" (Gal 1:14). He adds a few more autobiographical details: "[I was] circumcised on the eighth day, a member of the people of Israel, of the tribe of Benjamin, a Hebrew born of Hebrews; as to the law, a Pharisee; as to zeal, a persecutor of the church; as to righteousness under the law, blameless" (Phil 3:5–6). Taken together, these two passages reveal that Paul's ancestors were part of the legendary Israelite tribe of Benjamin (the tribe of Saul, ancient Israel's first king), that Paul himself was faithful in keeping the precepts of Jewish law from infancy (he was "blameless" when it came to the "law"), and that in his earlier life he had been an extremist zealot who tried to stamp out the early Christian movement, which means that he probably had been a member of the strictest sect of first-century Pharisaic Judaism. And as a Pharisee, Paul would have been an expert in Jewish law and customs and a scholar of the Hebrew Scriptures.

These biographical details are important because they help explain the many connections Paul makes between his Jewish sacred tradition and the gentile Christian churches he established. Paul frequently quoted or alluded to passages in the Hebrew Scriptures throughout his letters, thereby linking gentile Christians to the history of ancient Israel. He also used Israel's exodus story as a template when describing the effects of salvation. Paul writes that gentile Christians had been "slaves of sin" but that through Christ, they have now been "set free" (Rom 6:17–18; cf. Gal 5:1). This slave-freedom paradigm goes back to the exodus story, but Paul repurposes it when writing about the salvation of gentiles. Additionally, Paul refers to the Jewish messianic tradition when he calls Jesus of Nazareth the "Christ," a term that means "Messiah" or "Anointed One." And, of course, Paul uses language that is shaped by Jewish theology and practice to describe Christ's death on the cross. Paul calls the crucifixion a "sacrifice of atonement" (Rom 3:25)—an image that draws from the stipulations about animal sacrifices in Leviticus and also from the practice of offering animal sacrifices in the Jerusalem temple, which was still very much a part of Judaism during Paul's life.

PAUL AND COLONIALISM

It's also necessary to remember that Paul, like all first-century Jews in the Mediterranean world, resided in the Roman Empire. But Acts goes further and portrays Paul as a Roman citizen (Acts 22:28), a claim he never actually makes about himself in his letters, so it's historically uncertain whether he was indeed a citizen. Some New Testament scholars have begun referring to Paul as a "colonized apostle" to emphasize that Paul was a member of a conquered people.[25] A century before Paul wrote his letters, the Roman general Pompey led his legions on a conquest mission in the eastern Mediterranean, sacking the city of Jerusalem in the year 63 BCE. This permanently placed the region of Judea with its sacred city and temple under the jurisdiction of Roman governors and symbolically subjected Jews across the Mediterranean world—those who lived in the region of Judea and those who lived outside of Judea in the Diaspora—to the authority of Rome.

Being a conquered and colonized subject of Rome while also being proud of his ancestral Jewish heritage complicates Paul's identity. Some scholars refer to Paul's complex identity with a term drawn from postcolonial theory: *hybridity*.[26] According to Bill Ashcroft, Gareth Griffiths, and Helen Tiffin, postcolonialism analyzes "the effects of colonization on cultures and societies."[27] It is an approach to studying cultures that was first used by historians after the Second World War—a time in twentieth-century history when the centuries-long Western European colonial project throughout the world began to collapse in earnest. The aftermath of this collapse led scholars to begin examining the effects of Western colonialism on the psychology, identities, and cultures of the people under its influence.

Postcolonial theory is, in a way, a tailor-made approach to studying Paul—a Jewish colonized subject of the Roman

---

25. See Christopher D. Stanley, ed., *The Colonized Apostle: Paul through Postcolonial Eyes* (Minneapolis: Fortress, 2011).

26. See, for example, John W. Marshall, "Hybridity and Reading Romans," *Journal for the Study of the New Testament* 31, no. 2 (2008): 157–78.

27. Bill Ashcroft, Gareth Griffiths, and Helen Tiffin, *Post-colonial Studies: Key Concepts* (London: Routledge, 2000), 186.

Empire. When scholars describe Paul's identity with the term *hybridity*, they are borrowing a concept from horticulture and the crossbreeding of two distinct species to form a third or new hybrid.[28] Hybridity in culture studies emphasizes *both-and* and *neither-nor*.

My own academic work on this topic focuses on the first-century Jewish historian Titus Flavius Josephus.[29] Josephus's name is a Roman-Jewish blend, *both* Jewish *and* Roman but *neither* completely Jewish *nor* completely Roman. His name is structured according to the Roman convention of three names, or *tria nomina*, a distinction of Roman citizens. "Titus Flavius" indicates that Josephus was affiliated with the Flavian dynasty of emperors and that he was specifically named for the Roman general Titus, who sacked the city of Jerusalem in 70 CE. "Josephus" is a Judean name. Josephus had been a priest in the Jerusalem temple and had also been a general, fighting on the Judean side against the Romans when he defected to Rome. As the Roman legions were arrayed around the city of Jerusalem, Titus put the newly defected Josephus to work trying to convince his fellow Jews sitting atop the Jerusalem walls to surrender before the Roman army pressed its final assault on the city. In a stunning display of hybridity, Josephus walked the perimeter of the city just outside of the range of arrows hurled at him from Jews who viewed him as a traitor, and on behalf of the Roman army and its general, Josephus spoke in his native tongue to the Jews on the wall, pleading with them to surrender. A portion of the story is told as follows:

---

28. Ashcroft, Griffiths, and Tiffin, 118.

29. David A. Kaden, "Flavius Josephus and the *Gentes Devictae* in Roman Imperial Discourse: Hybridity, Mimicry, and Irony in the Agrippa II Speech (*Judean War* 2.345–402)," *Journal for the Study of Judaism* 42, nos. 4–5 (2011): 481–507.

> So Josephus went around the wall, and tried to find a place that was out of the reach of their darts, and yet within their hearing, and begged them, in many words, to spare themselves, to spare their country and their temple. . . . [He pleaded] that they must know the Roman power was invincible . . . ; for what part of the world is there that has escaped the Romans, unless it be such as are of no use due to violent heat or violent cold? And evident it is that fortune is on all hands gone over to [the Romans]; and that God when he had gone round the nations with this dominion, is now settled in Italy. . . . God [is] with them.[30]

After the war, Josephus was given Roman citizenship and the Roman names "Titus Flavius" to signify that he was now in the service of his Flavian imperial patrons. He was also given an apartment in Rome and a stipend from the imperial treasury that allowed him to end his career writing the books we still read today. The previous excerpt is extraordinary not only because Josephus is urging his fellow Jews to surrender by speaking to them in their native tongue but also because he claims that their God—the God whose temple is in Jerusalem—has blessed the Romans with worldwide dominion. God is "with them," he says. This is a hybrid form of language that is *both* Jewish *and* Roman but *neither* completely Jewish *nor* completely Roman. Josephus makes claims about the Romans that ancient Roman writers made about themselves—worldwide dominion, divine blessings on the empire, invincibility—but in mimicking this Roman imperial discourse, Josephus draws from his own Jewish theological tradition: it is the *Jewish* God,

---

30. Josephus, *Jewish War*, trans. H. J. Thackeray, vol. 3 (Cambridge, MA: Harvard University Press, 2014), 5.362–68 (italics original).

not the *Roman* gods, who has blessed the Roman Empire. This language is a hybrid effect of Josephus's complicated social location, and it provides a small window into how the blending and mixing of cultures, languages, and symbols produce variegated results. More importantly, in hybridizing Roman imperial discourse by claiming that the Jewish God, not the Roman gods, had blessed the empire, Josephus has delicately undercut a key claim of the empire. In the ancient world, if your side and your gods were successful in battle, it meant that the other side and its gods had been defeated. By this logic, Roman gods should be the most powerful in the Mediterranean world. Not so, claims Josephus. The Jewish God is still the true God even though God has now chosen to bless the Romans. It is a subtle destabilizing of Roman imperial propaganda, which claimed invincibility for both its legions and its gods.

PAUL THE JEW, PAUL THE ROMAN

Paul's letters do not provide nearly as dramatic an example of hybridity as that of Josephus, but they do offer a few instances that highlight Paul's own hybrid identity—*both* Jewish *and* Roman but *neither* completely Jewish *nor* completely Roman—and like Josephus, Paul also undercuts imperial propaganda. For example, when Paul writes about the geographic extent of his mission to bring the message of Christ's death and resurrection to the world in Romans 15:19 and 23–24, he speaks of beginning his mission in Jerusalem and then moving westward to the region of Illyricum—the area between Greece and Italy—then to Rome, and finally to Spain: "From Jerusalem and as far around as Illyricum I have fully proclaimed the good news of Christ. . . . But now, with no further place for me in these regions, I desire, as I have for many years, to come to you [in Rome] when I go to Spain." Jerusalem is Paul's springboard, his starting place, the center of his faith world because of its special place in Israel's history. But Paul's mission extends beyond Jerusalem to the ends of the Roman world. What's fascinating about the way Paul envisions the world of his day is how much his sense of geography is shaped by the Roman Empire. The empire extended westward from just east of Jerusalem, across the Mediterranean region, and ended in Spain. So when Paul writes about bringing the message of Christ's death and resurrection to the world of his day, he thinks in terms of Roman geography, from Jerusalem to Spain. In other words, Paul could, on the one hand, think like a Roman in that the world for him was the *Roman* world. On the other hand, Paul also thought like a Jew in that he viewed Jerusalem and not Rome itself as the most important city in the Roman world. Paul thus borrows Roman geography while subverting a key claim of the empire—namely, that the city of Rome was the center of the world. Romans 15:19, 23–24 is one of those tiny passages in Paul's letters that is easily skimmed over, but it offers a little window into Paul's hybrid identity.

Another example of hybridity in Paul's letters is his claim that Jesus is Lord. This statement is so fundamental to Christian doctrine that it might come as a surprise to learn that it is in fact a product of blended Jewish/Christian theological and Roman political discourses. The phrase itself is drawn in part from Jewish tradition embedded in the Hebrew Scriptures. In Psalm 100:3, the psalmist declares that "the Lord is God." And in Psalm 95:6–7, the psalmist says that "the Lord [is] our Maker! . . . He is our God." Drawing from this tradition, Paul connects Jesus with the Hebrew God, whose name is Yahweh— a word rendered in our English Bible as "Lord" (small caps).

Paul makes this connection explicit when he writes in 1 Corinthians 8:6, "For us there is one God, the Father . . . , and one Lord, Jesus Christ." Here Paul alludes to the first part of the Jewish Shema (*shema* comes from a Hebrew word that is translated into English as "hear"), a central prayer in Jewish monotheism: "Hear, O Israel: The Lord is our God, the Lord alone" (Deut 6:4). Scholar N. T. Wright has pointed out that in 1 Corinthians 8:6, Paul separated the names of God in the Shema by identifying "the Father" with "God" and "Jesus" with "the Lord," placing Jesus, says Wright, *at [the] very heart* of Jewish monotheism and incorporating Jesus into *the identity of Israel's God.*[31]

When Paul quotes what some scholars have said is an early Christian hymn in Philippians, he again connects Jesus with Yahweh:

Let the same mind be in you that was in Christ Jesus, who, though he was in the form of God, did not regard equality with God as something to be exploited, but emptied himself, taking the form of a slave, being born in human likeness. And being found in human form, he humbled himself and became obedient to the point of death—even death on a cross. Therefore God also highly exalted him and gave him the name that is above every name, so that *at the name of Jesus every knee should bend, in heaven and on earth and under the earth, and every tongue should confess that Jesus Christ is Lord, to the glory of God the Father.* (Phil 2:5–11; italics mine)

I'll return to the universalism implied in this passage, but for now, I want to focus on the italicized phrases of this hymn.

---

31. N. T. Wright, *Paul and the Faithfulness of God*, books 1–4 (Minneapolis: Fortress, 2013), book 2, 662, 684.

They are a direct reference to Isaiah 45:23, in which Yahweh says, "To me every knee shall bow, every tongue shall swear," which again implies that Paul has identified Jesus with Yahweh. Paul's Christology (his understanding of the person of Jesus Christ) thus forms an acorn of theology that would eventually become the oak tree of Trinitarianism centuries later in Christian history.

The final italicized phrase, *"every tongue should confess that Jesus Christ is Lord,"* is also significant because of its political ramifications. New Testament scholars have known for some time that the fundamental early Christian confession—Jesus is Lord—was not only or even primarily drawn from the theology of the Hebrew Scriptures; it was a political statement. Scholar Bruce Winter has documented the various points of connection between early Christian claims about Jesus and the claims made in Roman political propaganda about the emperors—in particular, the claim that Caesar is Lord. The first-century emperor Nero, for example, was referred to as "the Lord of all the world." And the emperor Domitian in the late first century was called "Lord and God." But "Christians," writes Winter, "confessed another as the Lord of the world."[32] Titles of Roman emperors also included the terms *son of god, savior,* and *benefactor,* all titles that New Testament writers ascribed to Jesus. So when Paul writes that Jesus is Lord, and when he claims in another place in his letters that confessing with one's lips that Jesus is Lord will lead one to salvation (Rom 10:9), he is not merely drawing from the Hebrew Scriptures to connect Jesus with Yahweh. He is also making a hybrid political statement: Jesus is both the manifestation of Yahweh and the true (Roman) Lord instead of Caesar—a statement that is *both* Jewish *and*

---

32. Winter, *Divine Honours,* 73.

Roman but *neither* completely Jewish *nor* completely Roman, a statement that relies on the weight of *both* Jewish theology *and* Roman political ideology for its meaning, and a statement that borrows from Roman political ideology in order to subvert it. By claiming that Jesus is Lord, early followers of Jesus like Paul were implying the inverse: Caesar is *not* Lord. Such a claim also meant that early Christians would face persecution at the hands of the Romans.

JESUS IS LORD— WHAT DOES IT MEAN TODAY?

This political edge is crucial for us to grasp as we try to decipher what the phrase "Jesus is Lord" means today, two millennia removed from its first articulation as a statement of faith. Because of the phrase's political implications in the first century, I find it amusing when some Christians today claim that churches shouldn't be political. There are certainly good reasons for churches not to be *partisan* (e.g., being partisan is against US tax code), but being *partisan* is not the same as being *political*. I once attended a General Synod gathering of the United Church of Christ (UCC) where this fine distinction was lost in a shockingly ironic way. I was a delegate at the time, and we were debating on the synod floor whether to issue a statement condemning the US war in Iraq. One person stood up to speak against such action, arguing that such a statement from a major American denomination would be too political—and churches, he argued, shouldn't delve into politics. He was standing at a microphone just a few feet from me, passionately making his case. The moment was surreal because the man was speaking while wearing a red baseball cap with the words *Jesus is Lord* emblazoned across the front. Clearly, he missed the irony. Speaking out against an unjust war—a war sold to the American people based on shady intelligence and the cynical manipulation of fear—is absolutely *political*, but it is not *partisan*. When we claim that Jesus is Lord, we are making a political statement that also implies the inverse: the Caesars of this world are *not* Lords.

Today's Caesars appear in the form of ideologies and actions that *degrade the human personality* (to borrow again from Dr. King). These actions include privileging profit over peacemaking, exalting the magic of the free market while casting aside the casualties of capitalism, viewing the world as a zero-sum game with winners and losers instead of as a human community of interconnection, succumbing to cynicism instead of living into the hope of love, promoting hate instead of compassion, and manipulating the so-called culture wars to enact oppressive policies. Being Caesar today could be as simple as sliding down the church pew away from the homeless person who just sat down. Basically, the Caesars of today, like the Caesars of old, divide the world into *us* and *them*. Ancient Caesars divided the world into the victorious (us) and the conquered (them). Today's Caesars might say, "*We* make a profit waging war while *they* become collateral damage; *we* take advantage of the market while *they* live paycheck to paycheck without health insurance; *we* are the winners, and *they* are the losers; *we* want a clean church with shiny people, which means *they* are not welcome."

To claim that Jesus is Lord and Caesar is not is to lay hold of a different way of being in the world, to see the world through a different set of lenses, to catch a glimpse of a different vision, the vision of Jesus. The statement "Jesus is Lord" should never become a bludgeon that clubs people of other religions or of no religion into submitting to Jesus. It should never be used in the way one of my evangelical seminary professors used it when he smugly said during class in answer to a student's question about other religions, "Well, Paul did say that *every knee will bow and every tongue will confess that Jesus is Lord*, so all people will eventually submit to Jesus, even if they do so in hell when it's too late!" He said this with a smirk. A ridiculous statement like this says more about the speaker and interpreter than it does about Paul, the writer.

The statement "Jesus is Lord" should instead be interpreted in a compassionate way, a way that *uplifts human personality*. Read in this way, the statement functions as a symbol to declare that the way of Jesus, according to Paul, is the way to a life lived compassionately, lovingly, and inclusively. Maybe this is what Paul was getting at when he wrote in Philippians 3:20 that our citizenship status derives its origin from a different place, a different state of mind. Our citizenship is heavenly, wrote Paul. The Greek word he uses, which our Bible renders into English as *citizenship* or *commonwealth*, is a political term. This commonwealth is not a physical place with borders and boundaries, nor is it a country way up in the sky far removed from any real-world, material relevance. It's a mindset that undercuts the claims of the world's Caesars by empowering Christians to live into the vision of Jesus, who taught his followers to pray, "Your kingdom come. Your will be done, on earth as it is in heaven" (Matt 6:10). Heavenly citizenship is a symbolic way of declaring that the true "empire" is not the one with its capital in Rome (or Washington, DC) but the one that is modeled on the way of Jesus. Jesus spoke of loving enemies and blessing the poor. He proclaimed a message of liberation for the oppressed, and he showcased what a life of compassion—God's life—looked like in flesh and blood. When Jesus sat beside the Samaritan woman at the well as recounted in the Gospel of John, for example, he modeled this boundary-crossing, compassionate way of life. He had a conversation with her and treated her as a human being instead of as an object. In contrast to the way of Caesar, Jesus treated her as an "us" instead of as a "them." It's instructive that after the disciples of Jesus returned from an errand, they were, according to John, "astonished that [Jesus] was speaking with a woman" (John 4:27). By just sitting and talking with her, Jesus crossed both an ethnic and a religious barrier in that she was a Samaritan. And because she was a woman, Jesus also crossed a gender barrier. Such a compassionate way of life could be called revolutionary when viewed from the vantage point of the world's Caesars.

PAUL'S MISSION

There is no evidence that Saint Paul knew about this story in John's Gospel. Indeed, Paul's letters seem, to put it mildly, disinterested in the life and teaching of Jesus. Paul never refers to the miracles of Jesus in his letters, and he never draws from the teachings of Jesus when offering moral guidance to gentile Christians. Instead, he focuses almost exclusively on the significance of Christ's death and resurrection. Why this is the case is a mystery. Perhaps Paul hadn't heard stories about the life of Jesus—the gospels weren't written until at least a decade or more after Paul's death. Or perhaps Paul knew about the life and teaching of Jesus but saw the cross and empty tomb as more important. Who can know for sure? Probing the motives of a two-thousand-year-old writer can be a dicey business, but it is clear that Paul's encounter with the risen Christ was world changing and paradigm shifting; he calls it God's special revelation to him (see Gal 1:12, 16). And according to scholar E. P. Sanders, this transformational encounter actually created problems for Paul.[33] Prior to meeting the risen Christ, Paul was probably quite happy in his Judaism. He "advanced in Judaism beyond many among [his] people," he was "zealous for the traditions of [his] ancestors" (Gal 1:14), and he was "blameless" (Phil 3:6) in keeping the precepts of the law of Moses, as he states in the letters of Galatians and Philippians. In other words, Paul was doing just fine as a faithful Jew before he met Jesus. Paul also almost certainly assumed that the promises of God sprinkled throughout the Hebrew Scriptures about the salvation of gentiles (non-Jews) would involve them coming in some way *to* Israel for their blessing. Isaiah 60:1–3 declares to the people of Israel, "Arise, shine; for your light has come, and the glory of the Lord has risen upon you. For darkness shall cover the earth, and thick darkness the peoples; but the Lord will arise upon you, and his glory will appear over you. Nations shall come to your light, and kings to the brightness of your dawn." Just how the nations (gentiles) would "come to your light" was a matter of dispute in the Judaism of Paul's day, and no doubt Paul had certain, settled views about this. But when he met Jesus Christ, his world was rocked. Instead of gentiles coming *to* Israel for salvation, Paul came to believe that God had commissioned *him* to "proclaim [Christ] among the Gentiles" (Gal 1:16). *He* was to take light *to* the nations in a reversal of Isaiah 60; and, as we saw previously, these nations were in Paul's mind the individual nations that comprised the Roman Empire. This tectonic shift in Paul's thinking was sparked by his encounter with the risen Christ: Christ was God's new solution to the salvation of gentiles—a solution that came as a complete surprise to Paul, who was forced back to the drawing board

---

33. E. P. Sanders, *Paul and Palestinian Judaism: A Comparison of Patterns of Religion* (Minneapolis: Fortress, 1977), 68.

of his faith to try to make sense of this new paradigm. E. P. Sanders calls it a "solution to plight" paradigm shift for Paul because he had to come to grips with the new reality that the instrument God was using to save gentiles (the solution) was a crucified messiah—a messiah subjected to the most terrifying form of execution at the hands of the Roman state, a political sentence—and further, that he himself was to be the messenger of this new reality.[34] Perhaps this earth-shaking transformation is the main reason that Paul focuses in his letters on the death and resurrection of Christ instead of on Christ's miracles and teachings—Paul was personally transformed by the *risen* Christ, and he came to believe that the *death* of Christ on the cross was God's mechanism for saving gentiles.

EXCURSUS: PAUL AND ANTI-JUDAISM

I have tried to be precise when speaking about the aim of Paul's mission as a follower of Jesus. I have spoken about Paul's mission as a mission to the *gentiles* instead of as a mission to the whole world—the world of gentiles *and* Jews. This is in part because Paul himself makes this distinction in Galatians 1 and 2: He was chosen by God, he says, to "proclaim [Christ] among the nations [i.e., gentiles]" (Gal 1:16). He went to Jerusalem to explain to church leaders there "the gospel that I proclaim among the Gentiles" (Gal 2:2), and he makes the surprising claim that he "had been entrusted with the gospel for the uncircumcised [i.e., gentiles], just as Peter had been entrusted with the gospel for the circumcised [i.e., Jews]" (Gal 2:7). This means *two gospels* were being preached by the earliest followers of Jesus, *two different messages* (I'll return to this later). And it

---

34. Sanders, 482.

means that everything Paul writes in his letters is intended for gentiles, *not* for both Jews and gentiles. Whether he's writing about ethics or salvation or the person of Christ, Paul's primary audience—the people he is interpreting the Hebrew Scriptures and the story of Jesus for—comprises gentiles, *not* Jews.

The tendency in Christian history (as we saw earlier in Martin Luther's vile treatise *On the Jews and Their Lies*) has been to universalize Paul's language and apply it to both gentiles *and* Jews, turning Paul into Christianity's first anti-Semite (or, to be more historically accurate, "anti-Jew"). So, for example, when Paul writes about the Jewish law (the law of Moses embedded in the first five books of the Bible), he often says very negative things that no good Jew would say about their ancestral faith tradition. Paul says the law increases awareness of sin (Rom 3:20), it brings God's wrath (Rom 4:15), it multiplies sin (Rom 5:20), it enslaves (Rom 7:6; Gal 5:1), and it leads to death (1 Cor 15:56). If Paul was so proud of his ancestral Jewish heritage, how could he write such things? Most writers and thinkers throughout Christian history have concluded that Paul's encounter with the risen Christ transformed him so thoroughly that he rejected the Judaism of his past and came to see it as part of a "ministry of death" (2 Cor 3:7). In effect, so this line of thought goes, Paul shows us that Judaism is inferior to Christianity and thus has been superseded by it.

Paul is such a powerful thinker and he holds such a large place in the Christian imagination that this anti-Jewish line of thought has unleashed untold devastation in history. Indeed, it isn't a stretch to connect this line of thought to the second-century Marcionite theology that viewed the God of the Old Testament as inferior to the God of the New Testament; it isn't a stretch to connect this line of thought to the epithet "Christ killers," a charge leveled against Jews throughout history.

It isn't a stretch to connect this line of thought to the Rhineland massacres of the First Crusade in the eleventh century, which targeted Jewish communities. It isn't a stretch to connect this line of thought to Martin Luther's anti-Jewish treatise during the Protestant Reformation. And it isn't a stretch to connect this line of thought to the gas chambers of Auschwitz.[35] If interpreting Paul's letters says more about the interpreters than it does about Paul, then Christianity has anti-Semitism in its DNA, something we modern, progressive Christians need to be honest about if we want to address it. Scholar Lloyd Gaston once wrote, "It is the task of exegesis after Auschwitz precisely to expose the explicit or implicit anti-Judaism inherent in the Christian tradition, including the New Testament itself."[36] To put this another way, How might we progressive Christians interpret Paul in a way that *uplifts human personality*, including especially *Jewish* human personality?

TWO GOSPELS

Here we can return to Paul's fundamental mission of preaching the gospel to gentiles rather than Jews. As the apostle to the gentiles, almost everything Paul wrote in his letters was intended for this ethnic group. So when Paul writes negative things about the law of Moses, he's intending these statements to describe how *gentiles relate to the Jewish law* and *not* how Jews

---

35. See Rosemary Ruether, *Faith and Fratricide: The Theological Roots of Anti-Semitism* (Eugene, OR: Wipf & Stock, 1995).

36. Lloyd Gaston, *Paul and the Torah* (Eugene, OR: Wipf & Stock, 1987), 2.

relate to their own law.[37] *For gentiles*, the law increases awareness of sin, brings God's wrath, enslaves, and leads to death. This is all hyperbolic language, and none of these statements apply to Jews. If we interpret Paul in a way that *uplifts human personality*, it is clear that he had no problem with Judaism or Jews. He was himself a faithful Jew and, as several scholars have pointed out, remained so throughout his entire life. Paul's encounter with the risen Christ convinced him that the way *gentiles* could enter the Abrahamic family of faith was through Christ.

This brings us back to the two gospels that Paul mentions in Galatians 2. Paul preaches one gospel to the gentiles while Peter preaches another to Jews. Paul outlines these two gospels in Romans 15:8–9: "For I tell you that Christ has become a servant of the circumcised [i.e., Jews] on behalf of the truth of God in order that he might confirm the promises given to the patriarchs, and in order that the Gentiles might glorify God for his mercy." The gospel to the Jews is that God has fulfilled the "promises given to the patriarchs." Paul is likely referring to the promise God made to Abram (before his name was changed to Abraham) that through Abram's descendants, God would bless all the families of the earth (Gen 12:3). The open question in the Judaism of Paul's day concerned the means by which God would fulfill this promise. After meeting the risen Christ, Paul became convinced that God was fulfilling this promise through the death and resurrection of Christ. Put differently, Christ is the *way* into the family of Abraham—the way of blessing and salvation—*for gentiles*.

The gospel to the gentiles—the gospel that Paul proclaims— invites the gentiles to join the family of Abraham and thus

---

37. See John G. Gager, *Reinventing Paul* (New York: Oxford University Press, 2000).

become part of God's own people by means of adoption (Rom 8:15). They can do this, says Paul, "apart from law" (Rom 3:21)—that is, they do not need to become converts to Judaism in order to become part of Abraham's family. Gentile males do not need to be circumcised, and gentile men and women do not need to keep a kosher diet, observe Jewish festivals, or keep the Sabbath. They do not need to observe the laws and customs that mark out the biological children of Abraham (Jews) because God has provided a different way for them to enter Abraham's family, the way of faith in Christ. Indeed, if gentiles were to adopt Jewish laws and customs, they would cease being gentiles and would become Jews, thereby nullifying God's promise to save gentiles *as* gentiles. Incidentally, the main reason why Paul is so furious in his letter to the Galatians is because the Galatian Christians had begun to follow Jewish laws and customs, thinking that these "works" were needed in addition to faith in Christ in order to be part of Abraham's family. This for Paul is unacceptable because it subverts the plan of God, which aims to save gentiles through Christ and not, as he says, through "works of the law" (Gal 2:16).

Yet Paul is clear that Jews are the natural, biological children of Abraham. They are *already* part of Abraham's family, and the observance of their laws and customs (circumcision, festivals, kosher diet, Sabbath) maintains this special covenantal status. Jews are chosen and beloved, writes Paul, and "the gifts and the calling of God are irrevocable" (Rom 11:28b–29). God treats the descendants of Israel on their own special and ancient covenantal terms, which Paul recognizes when he writes that "all Israel will be saved" (Rom 11:26). In other words, *Jews do not need to convert to Christianity in order to be saved* because Christ is not their *way* into Abraham's family. They are born naturally into this family, while gentiles are adopted into this family by modeling the faith of Abraham. Abraham proved that he "believed the Lord" (Gen 15:6) when he trusted God's promises. Using the example of Abraham as a template, Paul argues that "those who believe [i.e., gentiles] are [also] the descendants of Abraham" (Gal 3:7). So Paul can say that God's promises are for "all [Abraham's] descendants, *not only* to the adherents of the law [i.e., Jews] *but also* to those who share the faith of Abraham [i.e., gentiles]" (Rom 4:16; italics mine). Paul is thus arguing for two ways into Abraham's family: the Jewish way of being born naturally into this family and the gentile way of having faith in Christ. Scholar Pamela Eisenbaum summarizes this two-ways theology well when she writes, "What was accomplished by Jesus's death was the reconciliation of *Gentiles* to God, and that . . . is all Paul ever claimed Jesus accomplished. In other words, Jesus's death is not intended for the salvation of the whole world but rather just for the salvation of Gentiles. . . . Paul did not have a problem with Jews, Judaism, or Jewish law."[38]

Paul was writing almost six centuries before the appearance of Islam in religious history. I would bet—and this is just a hunch—that had Paul been around when Muhammad first recited the Qur'an, and given the significance he accords to the family of Abraham in his letters, Paul may have included Muslims among those born *into* Abraham's family, since Muslims trace their religious lineage to Ishmael, the first of Abraham's sons. For those of us who still revere Paul and who are committed to reading the Bible in a way that *uplifts human personality,* we might then conclude that there are now at least *three* ways

---

38. Pamela Eisenbaum, "Jewish Perspectives: A Jewish *Apostle to the Gentiles,*" in *Studying Paul's Letters,* 142.

into the Abrahamic family: the Jewish way, the Muslim way, and the gentile way.

Some Christian readers may cringe at this argument. Some might even call it heresy because (for them) it seems to diminish the singular importance of Christ's death on the cross to secure salvation. I would respond with a few questions: Why do you see it as heresy? What about this perspective is offensive to you? How might your assumptions about what is true be affecting your reaction? How might you interpret Paul's own statements differently? Why might you interpret Paul's statements differently? And keep in mind that our interpretations say more about us than they do about Paul. The interpretation of Paul I've offered does not in any way diminish the historic confessions about Christ's divine-human identity (see the Nicaean and Chalcedonian creeds). It only speaks to what God intends for the family of Abraham. And just because we're reading Paul in this way doesn't necessarily mean that every other New Testament writer can be read in this way; each New Testament book presents its own challenge for interpreters who are committed to *uplifting human personality*. The letter to the Hebrews, for example, seems to see Christianity as taking the place of Judaism, which the writer sees as a sort of precursor to the main Christian event. The Gospel of John says that "the Jews"—a phrase that seems to make no exceptions, even though I think it's a terrible translation of the Greek— are hostile to Jesus and ultimately instrumental in bringing about his crucifixion (John 18:38b–40). Revelation refers to the Jewish place of worship as a "synagogue of Satan" (Rev 2:9; 3:9). And the Gospel of Peter (a noncanonical gospel) implies strongly that the Jews actually carried out the crucifixion. Interpretations that *uplift human personality* in each of these books will look different, even if such interpretations lead the interpreters to disagree with the ancient writer(s). By interpreting Paul in a more compassionate way, we are trying to counter the anti-Semitism and anti-Judaism of our Christian texts and traditions and also destabilize the majority discourse in Christian history that has viewed Paul as the first to break decisively with his ancestral heritage.

Those who are familiar with Paul's writings may be cycling in their minds through a Rolodex of passages from his letters—possibly under the influence of certain Protestant Reformers—that they think disprove this argument. I can only point such savvy readers to the scholarly literature for answers to their questions. The best place to start in my opinion is with John Gager's book *Reinventing Paul*.[39] I also want to reemphasize that the central argument of this chapter is that each of us must decide whether we will read Scripture in a way that *degrades* or *uplifts* human personality. Reading Paul in a way that *uplifts* human personality turns him into one of the most inclusive, progressive, and grace-filled writers in early Christianity. His entire mission was to welcome gentile outsiders into the Abrahamic family of faith. But if we take seriously Paul's claim that every knee will bow and every tongue confess that Jesus is Lord, we must ask further questions. What about those gentiles who practice non-Abrahamic religions? What about those who practice no religion at all? Does Paul's theology have universalist implications?

PAUL'S UNIVERSALISM

Paul's complicated identity makes his letters difficult to systematize in part because he writes to gentiles from a Jewish

---

39. Gager, *Reinventing Paul.*

perspective, borrowing both from the symbols and language of his ancestral heritage and also from the worlds of political Rome and Greco-Roman culture. He also claims to have shifting identities—he claims to be "all things to all people," a Jew for Jews, a gentile for gentiles (1 Cor 9:22b). Paul doesn't fit neatly into accepted categories—some scholars have even called him queer for this reason (this is not a statement about Paul's sexual orientation as much as it is a statement about Paul's ability to traverse human-made categories). His shifting identities did, however, enable him to be quite effective in expanding the early Christian movement to what philosopher Peter Sloterdijk calls the "global scale."[40] Nevertheless, I think Paul wrestled at times with the explosive and expansive implications of his theology.

On the one hand, Paul can seem restrictive when he writes about the means by which non-Abrahamic gentiles are saved. He talks about the necessity of faith in Jesus Christ (Rom 3:22). He lists a series of wrongdoers who "will not inherit the kingdom of God": "fornicators, idolaters, adulterers, male prostitutes, sodomites, thieves, the greedy, drunkards, revilers, robbers" (1 Cor 6:9–10; I'll return to the topic of vice lists in the next chapter). Perhaps Paul didn't know that Jesus ate and fellowshipped with "tax collectors and sinners" (Matt 9:10). Had he known, maybe he would've been less harsh. Maybe he wouldn't have written this section of 1 Corinthians 6 at all. It's also possible that some of these restrictive passages in Paul's letters are residuals from his earlier life as a fundamentalist Pharisee. Put crudely, you can take the Pharisee out of fundamentalism, but it's hard to take fundamentalism out of the Pharisee. Paul was

---

40. Peter Sloterdijk, *God's Zeal: The Battle of the Three Monotheisms*, trans. Wieland Hoban (Cambridge: Polity, 2009), 30.

only human after all, and we humans are powerfully driven to create boundaries that demarcate insiders and outsiders.

On the other hand, Paul's own theology about Christ's death and resurrection led him to make statements that sound universalist (i.e., all people will be saved)—statements that break down all barriers between people and treat every human being and all of creation as beloved of God. In Romans 3:23–24, Paul writes, "Since all [gentiles] have sinned and fall short of the glory of God; they are now justified by his grace as a gift, through the redemption that is in Christ Jesus." If *all* have sinned, then *all* are justified (i.e., placed in right standing with God = saved). Similarly, in Romans 5:18, when Paul says that the sin of Adam in Genesis infects all of gentile humanity, he says the death of Christ leads to "life for all." If "all" have sinned, then, according to Paul's own logic, "all" are saved through Christ. When it comes to the planet itself, Paul writes in Romans 8:19 that the entire "creation waits" to be set free—his vision is of a salvation that encompasses all people and the entire planet. Likewise, 2 Corinthians 5:19 speaks of God "reconciling the world [the cosmos]." In Romans 11:32, Paul writes that God will ultimately be "merciful to all," which implies universal salvation. In 1 Corinthians 15:22, Paul writes again about Adam's sin and Christ's death, stating that "as all die in Adam, so all will be made alive in Christ." If "all" gentile humanity dies because of Adam's sin in Genesis, then again, according to Paul's own logic, "all" will be made alive (i.e., saved) because of Christ's death on the cross. And in the disputed letters—the letters we're not certain Paul actually wrote—this spirit of universalism is present. Ephesians 1:10 speaks of God's plan "to gather up all things" (i.e., to bring all things—people and planet—to the completion of salvation). And Colossians 1:20 states that "God was pleased to reconcile to himself all things, whether on earth or in heaven, by making peace through the blood of [Christ's] cross." The phrase "all things" means just what it says: nothing—no person and no part of the planet—will ultimately be left outside of God's saving intention.

The questions for us as we read Paul's letters two thousand years after he wrote them are as follows: Which passages and interpretations will we privilege? Which passages and interpretations will help us be more compassionate? Which passages and interpretations will help us *uplift human personality*? If we privilege the universalist and inclusivist perspectives when interpreting Philippians 2, then we can read Paul's statement about every knee bowing and every tongue confessing that Jesus is Lord as a symbolic way of declaring that *every* person is beloved of God.[41] The vision of Philippians 2 is a universalistic vision even if the specific language is distinctively Christian and Christ-centered.[42]

I find it particularly interesting that if Philippians 2:5–11 was originally a hymn (as I noted earlier)—perhaps the first ever written by early Christians—then the earliest followers of Jesus, including Paul, worshipped together by singing into being a progressive vision of the world where *all people* would be included and welcomed at the table of salvation.

---

41. In Romans 14:11, Paul quotes the same verse from Isaiah 45 about knees bowing and tongues confessing that he quotes in Philippians 2. Romans 14 is a context of judgment, Philippians 2 of salvation. *Uplifting human personality* in Romans 14 will, accordingly, look different than it does when interpreting Philippians 2.

42. For a recent treatment of universalism, see David Bentley Hart, *That All Shall Be Saved: Heaven, Hell, and Universal Salvation* (New Haven, CT: Yale University Press, 2019).

CONCLUSION

Is Paul still relevant today? His letters are ancient, densely written, easily misunderstood, and even more easily misapplied to situations he could never have imagined. We can't know for sure how Paul would react to see that his letters have been used in Christian history to oppress, dehumanize, and mistreat human beings. I think Paul would be horrified. I think this because I recognize that all biblical interpretation is an exercise in ethics—our interpretations have moral consequences. So we must *choose* how to apply Paul's letters today. *We* decide how Paul will speak today. What *we* hear Paul saying in his ancient letters says more about us than it does about Paul. Will we interpret Paul's letters in a way that *degrades* or *uplifts* human personality?

5

DESIGNING A LOVING AND PROGRESSIVE CHURCH WHERE NO ONE IS OUT

The basic problem is that people are so ingenious at adapting to inconvenient situations that they are often not even aware that they are doing so: they sit on their seat belts, write their PINs on their hands, hang their jackets on doorknobs, and chain their bicycles to park benches.

—Tim Brown, *Change by Design*

Something or someone is made sacred by ritual.

—Jonathan Z. Smith, *To Take Place*

Love pushes us beyond duty, rather than stopping there, and acts when we don't know for sure what the ethical thing to do is. If the ethical question is, "What must be done?" love adds, "I will do more." If our ethical compass is not able to give us a clear direction to travel, love sets out the way.

—Peter Rollins, *The Orthodox Heretic and Other Impossible Tales*

What might it mean to be drawn into meanings that, in some profound sense, shatter us? This is what it means to love.
—Christian Wiman, *My Bright Abyss*

REDESIGNING CHURCH

In his book *Change by Design*, Tim Brown, CEO of the design firm IDEO, outlines the features of innovative design thinking.[1] These features were put into practice during a 1999 episode of the ABC News show *Nightline*, which challenged IDEO designers to create a new kind of shopping cart using the principles of innovative design thinking. IDEO describes the process their designers pursued during the challenge and the results they achieved. First, the process: "IDEO created a new shopping cart concept, considering issues such as maneuverability, shopping behavior, child safety, and maintenance cost. The [ABC] show concentrated on IDEO's design process, recording as a multidisciplinary team brainstormed, researched, prototyped, and gathered user feedback on a design that went from idea to a working appearance model in four days." Then the result:

The nestable steel frame [on the new shopping cart] lacks sides and a bottom to deter theft, and holds removable plastic baskets to increase shopper flexibility, help protect goods, and provide a method to promote brand awareness. A dual child seat uses a swing-up tray for a play surface, and a hole provides a secure spot for a cup of coffee or a bunch of carnations. One of the unique—and potentially patentable—features of the cart is the design of its steerable back wheels.

---

1. Tim Brown, *Change by Design: How Design Thinking Transforms Organizations and Inspires Innovation* (New York: Harper Business, 2009).

Normally fixed straight for stability and familiarity, an easy sideways effort allows the wheels to turn left or right. Pushing the cart forward puts the wheels straight again.[2]

A picture of this newly designed shopping cart can be seen on IDEO's website. But IDEO has done more than reimagine shopping carts. It has designed all sorts of things: they helped Verizon create the mobile Verizon Explorer Lab to excite young students about possibilities in the STEM field; they helped Bowdoin College become more efficient at reading and processing college applications; they teamed up with the Center for NYC Neighborhoods to create FloodHelpNY.org to help New Yorkers in neighborhoods vulnerable to flooding become more educated about risks and prepare ahead; they worked with a company called Innova to redesign curricula, teacher training, and even school buildings for K–12 children in Peru; and more than a decade ago, they helped HBO become one of the first companies to offer on-demand service to viewers—something we all take for granted now. The list of successful and groundbreaking IDEO redesigns is staggering.

IDEO's design thinking solves problems by observing human behavior, the "ingenious" ways, as Tim Brown calls them, that people solve everyday problems, like sitting on their seat belts, writing PINs on their hands, hanging their jackets on doorknobs, and chaining their bicycles to park benches. But design thinking goes deeper than merely solving everyday problems; it looks for "rule-breaking, game-changing, paradigm-shifting breakthroughs that leave us scratching our heads and

---

2. "Reimagining the Shopping Cart," IDEO, accessed February 26, 2021, https://tinyurl.com/y6cramh6.

wondering why nobody ever thought of them before."[3] Tim Brown is fond of quoting Henry Ford, who once said, "If I'd asked my customers what they wanted, they'd have said 'a faster horse.'"[4] Ford went on to mass-produce the first affordable automobiles.

What if we undertook an IDEO-type redesign of church? Although there have always been progressives in Christian history (e.g., egalitarians, abolitionists, preachers of a social gospel, feminists, liberation theologians, civil rights activists, etc.), my main point throughout this book and now in this final chapter is that twenty-first-century progressive Christianity offers the kind of game-changing and paradigm-shifting, IDEO-type breakthrough that is both an "organizing principle" (to borrow again from Ross Douthat, cited in chapter 1), anchored in a critical interpretation of the Bible and Christian tradition, and also a way to live more compassionately and intentionally today for the betterment of humanity.[5] Progressive Christianity is a key part of what scholar Diana Butler Bass calls the "Fourth Great Awakening" in this country—an awakening that takes the religious past and makes it "humane in the service of the global community."[6]

In the previous chapters, I have described a version of progressive Christianity that is inspired by prophetic dreams of justice and peace (chapter 1). It sees relationship, community, and connection as aspects of the divine, allowing us to experience God in the midst of our interactions with people and the planet (chapter 2). It sees in Jesus an example of boundary-breaking

---

3. Brown, *Change by Design*, 40.
4. Brown, 46.
5. Douthat, "Save the Mainline."
6. Butler Bass, *Christianity after Religion*, 239.

love and invites us to live more fully into his message and way of life (chapter 3). And it reads Paul's letters and all of Scripture in a way that uplifts human personality, as resources for celebrating diversity and inclusivity (chapter 4). The Bible and Christian tradition are places to start a conversation about how to live in a compassionate and loving way. They are like the foundation of a great house. People don't live in unfinished basements with no house or roof above. The foundation, rooted to the earth, gives stability and grounding, but it's the floors above that provide the space for living. As anyone who owns a house knows, the interior and exterior structures are in need of regular maintenance. Homeowners also often change the furniture, the artwork on the walls, the paint color in the rooms, the trim along the floors, and the floors themselves, and sometimes they renovate entire sections—likewise when it comes to a great religious tradition such as Christianity. We don't live in the unfinished foundation of the Nicene fourth century, the Chalcedonian fifth century, or even the Pauline first century; we draw from the past, we set our feet on the foundation they laid, and then we build, renovate, improve, and redesign. Christians have always treated their past in this way. One need only read, for example, the edicts of the five Lateran councils from the twelfth century to the sixteenth century or read the works of the Protestant Reformers to see how interpretations of Scripture and tradition get redesigned to meet current needs. The version of progressive Christianity that I am outlining is another example of this same process, but unlike many of its Christian forebears, progressive Christianity is not trying to set up boundary markers that demarcate insiders and outsiders, true believers and heretics, orthodoxies and heterodoxies. This version of Christianity instead reinterprets Scripture and tradition in order to demolish such false binaries and invites us to privilege those features of our past that can help us live more compassionately in the present and future.

AN OPEN-CONCEPT DESIGN

At one of the memorial services for Matthew Shepard—a gay man who was murdered in October 1998—Rev. Tom Troeger told a story in his eulogy about a game he would play with his friends as a child. Half of the children would form a circle, lock hands, and face outward. The other half of the children were outside of the circle. The ones in the circle would chant, "You're out! You're out! You can't come in. You're out! You're out! You can't come in!" The children outside of the circle would then rush toward it as hard as they could and try to break through. Troeger admits that he always seemed to be on the outside, unable to break through, until one day, a girl named Louise winked at him as the children chanted, "You're out! You're out! You can't come in." When Troeger rushed toward the circle to break through, Louise dropped the hand of the boy next to her and Troeger got in. The boy next to Louise was outraged, saying, "You can't do that! If you do that, *everyone* will get in!" Troeger ended his sermon by saying, "God is like Louise."[7]

One way to redesign church in an IDEO-type way is to imagine it as a place where *no one is out*. Such a redesign goes beyond the bland "All Are Welcome!" words adorning nearly every church sign across America. To say and really mean that *no one is out* is to make a far more explosive claim: it erases the

---

7. John A. Stroman, *Out of the Whirlwind: First Lesson Sermons for Sundays after Pentecost (Last Third), Cycle B* (Lima, OH: CSS, 1999), 41.

distinction between the sacred and the profane. Quoting poet Wendell Berry, Franciscan friar Richard Rohr once said, "There are not sacred and profane things, places, and moments. There are only *sacred* things and *desecrated* things, places, and moments. . . . It is one sacred universe, and we are all part of it."[8] He calls this perspective an "incarnational worldview." It is, he says, "the profound recognition of the presence of the divine in literally 'every thing' and 'every one,'" which means that identifying certain people or things as sacred while identifying others as secular or profane creates a false separation.[9] Seeing the divine in all things means that, strictly speaking, nothing in God's universe can be profane. Nothing is *out*—which is another way of saying that God's grace has no limits; it extends to all of creation and to all people, even to those people who seem least deserving of it. If grace were deserved, it wouldn't be grace.

THE SACRED, THE SECULAR, AND THE SURVEYS

The categories of the sacred and the secular or profane have occupied the minds of generations of cultural anthropologists, sociologists, scholars of religion, church historians, biblical interpreters, and theologians. Augustine of Hippo's early fifth-century work *City of God* divided the world into elect and pagan, sacred and profane. Augustine attempted to shift blame away from Christians for the sacking of Rome in 410 CE by

---

8. Richard Rohr, *Just This: Prompts and Practices for Contemplation* (London: SPCK, 2017), 69.

9. Rohr, *Universal Christ*, 18.

King Alaric's Visigoths toward Rome's paganism, which opened the door, he argued, to immorality and the ultimate fall of the city. More recently, scholar of religion Mircea Eliade sharply distinguished between sacred things and profane things, seeing both categories as "two [different] modes of being in the world" that shape how human beings treat the spaces in which they dwell, view time, share stories, experience nature, and even live life itself: "[The religious person] always believes that there is an absolute reality, *the sacred*, which transcends this world but manifests itself in this world, thereby sanctifying it and making it real. He [*sic*] further believes that life has a sacred origin. . . . Modern nonreligious man assumes a new existential situation; he regards himself solely as the subject and agent of history, and he refuses to appeal to transcendence. . . . Just as nature is the product of a progressive secularization of the cosmos as the work of God, profane man is the result of a desacralization of human existence."[10] Eliade argues that religious forms and language are so pervasive that they continue to structure the lives of "profane man," but his distinction between the sacred and the profane and his comment about the "desacralization of human existence" illustrate an idea that is axiomatic for many in our time—namely, that the world (or at least the Western world) is becoming less religious. The term for this is *secularization*, what scholars Pippa Norris and Ronald Inglehart in their book *Sacred and Secular* have called "the conventional wisdom" about "the death of religion."[11]

The specter of secularization haunts our interpretations of social-scientific research of religious life in the United States.

---

10. Mircea Eliade, *The Sacred and the Profane: The Nature of Religion*, trans. William R. Trask (London: Harcourt, 1987), 14, 202–4 (italics original).

11. Pippa Norris and Ronald Inglehart, *Sacred and Secular: Religion and Politics Worldwide* (Cambridge: Cambridge University Press, 2013), 3.

In 2015, the Pew Research Center published an eye-catching article, "US Public Becoming Less Religious," based on results from their 2014 Religious Landscape survey that asked thirty-five thousand American adults about their belief in God, prayer life, and attendance at religious services. The article called these beliefs and practices "key measures of what it means to be a religious person."[12] Pew has conducted follow-up surveys since 2014 and found that the United States is seeing a decline in the number of people who self-identify as Christian. From 2009 to 2019, the number of Americans who call themselves Christian decreased twelve percentage points from 77 percent to 65 percent, while the number of religiously unaffiliated—the "nones"—climbed from 17 percent to 26 percent of the US population.[13] The number of people who regularly attend religious services has also declined:

> Over the last decade, the share of Americans who say they attend religious services at least once or twice a month dropped by 7 percentage points, while the share who say they attend religious services less often (if at all) has risen by the same degree. In 2009, regular worship attenders (those who attend religious services at least once or twice a month) outnumbered those who attend services only occasionally or not at all by a 52%-to-47% margin. Today those figures are reversed; more Americans now say they attend

---

12. "U.S. Public Becoming Less Religious: Modest Drop in Overall Rates of Belief and Practice, but Religiously Affiliated Americans Are as Observant as Before," Pew Research Center, Washington, DC, November 3, 2015, https://tinyurl.com/yyh3lu36.

13. "In U.S., Smaller Share of Adults Identify as Christians, While Religious 'Nones' Have Grown," Pew Research Center, Washington, DC, October 16, 2019, https://tinyurl.com/y2eh2l2a.

religious services a few times a year or less (54%) than say they attend at least monthly (45%).[14]

These studies are useful for tracking how people self-identify—Christian or not—and how often they attend religious gatherings, but they do not prove that the country is becoming less religious or more secular.

The problem with words like *sacred, secular, profane, secularization,* and even the word *religion* itself is that they are laden with all sorts of baggage. Defining the word *religion* is especially perilous because of its ripple effects. Assumptions about what constitutes religious behavior—belief in God, prayer life, and attendance at religious services, according to Pew researchers—become markers that divide people into categories and actually create the conditions for concluding that the United States is becoming less religious and more secular. Defining religion as a set of beliefs and practices, usually including some personal belief in the supernatural, isolates a set of traits that *we* think mark out religious life. If a person does not fit within the confines of the definition, then *we* can conclude that they are nonreligious; and if enough people over time do not fit within the confines of this definition, then *we* can conclude that the society as a whole is becoming less religious. The way we define religion also shapes the ways we define terms like *secular* and *secularization.* If a group of people does not fit within a certain definition of religion, then they must be secular, and if enough of them over time do not fit within this definition,

---

14. "In U.S., Decline of Christianity Continues at a Rapid Pace: An Update on America's Changing Religious Landscape," Pew Research Center, Washington, DC, October 17, 2019, https://tinyurl.com/y54m8cjv.

then the society as a whole must be going through a process of secularization. Or so the story goes.

Scholars of religion have argued that defining religion as a set of beliefs and practices that incorporate the supernatural emerged fairly recently in Western history and is guided by an overwhelmingly Protestant and church-focused framework about what religion is supposed to be—a framework that has proven inadequate in explaining the diverse ways that people practice a thing we might call religion across cultures and times.[15] If religion is defined as a set of beliefs and practices involving the supernatural, then how would we classify self-proclaimed nontheist mainline Christians or atheist Jews or atheist Unitarian Universalists? They may all practice something that looks like religion and may even self-identify as religious, but are they religious if they claim to be materialists who don't believe in the supernatural? Similarly problematic is classifying something like the cultural practice of head-hunting among the Ilongots of the Philippines. Head-hunting involves rituals, beliefs, and customs that regulate Ilongot society—all traits that could be included in a definition of religion. But the Ilongots themselves seem to see head-hunting as distinct from their beliefs and practices that involve the supernatural.[16] Even the ancient Latin word *religio*, as scholar Brent Nongbri observes, "had a variety of meanings in antiquity [none of which] corresponds to the modern notion of religion" as something personal and belief oriented. "In the late Roman republic," he writes, "*religio*

---

15. See Brent Nongbri, *Before Religion: A History of a Modern Concept* (New Haven, CT: Yale University Press, 2013).

16. See Renato Rosaldo, *Ilongot Headhunting 1883–1974: A Study in Society and History* (Stanford, CA: Stanford University Press, 1980).

seems to have ranged from meaning simply 'rule' or 'worship practice' to 'excessive concern about the gods.'"[17]

The categories we use to classify and measure people and things are artificial. The categories we create and the traits we isolate to mark out those categories say more about us and our assumptions than they do about the people or things we are trying to classify. This is the case for categories like *sacred, secular, profane, secularization*, and *religion*; it's also the case for categories like *sinner, believer, heretic, progressive*, and so on. Questions to ask ourselves when creating a category are as follows: What am I trying to do with this category? Am I trying to find a thing called secularization in the world? Am I trying to divide people into categories of sacred and secular/profane? Am I trying to illuminate some aspect of human behavior that I think needs more attention? (By the way, this last question is how I'm treating the category of progressive Christianity.) If the categories we create say more about us than they do about the people or things we are trying to classify, then every category we use is doing some kind of work for us: defining, confining, dividing, concealing, combining, illuminating. Anthropologist Mary Douglas made a similar point after a cross-cultural study of rituals that deal with dirt and impurity. "There is no such thing as absolute dirt," she wrote. "It exists in the eye of the beholder."[18]

One way to view the categories we create is to see them not as identifying actual people or things in the world but merely as ways of looking at the world. Change how we define the category, and we can change our perspective. For example,

---

17. See Nongbri, *Before Religion*, 26, 28. For a provocative treatment of the problem of categories, see Jonathan Z. Smith, "Fences and Neighbors," in *Imagining Religion*, 1–18.

18. Mary Douglas, *Purity and Danger: An Analysis of Concept of Pollution and Taboo* (New York: Routledge, 2002), 3.

instead of seeing religion as a system of beliefs and practices that incorporate the supernatural, we might see religion more broadly as a way to make meaning in the world. As I mentioned earlier, Jonathan Z. Smith suggested that "religion is one mode of constructing worlds of meaning." It is, he said, "the quest" to create "'space' in which to meaningfully dwell."[19] No definition of religion is once and for all (and some would argue that even here the subtle Smith was not constructing a single definition), but this particular perspective spotlights the many ways that human beings make meaning. Participating in church life with beliefs and practices that incorporate the supernatural is only one way to make meaning. Practicing other religious traditions is another way to make meaning. Living one's life with the goal of accumulating as much money and wealth as possible is another way. Spending Sunday mornings playing golf instead of attending church might be another. Moving up the cultural ladder through career advances and social climbing might be another still. Trying to become a Jedi Knight or learning the spells of a Hogwarts wizard or witch might be others. Each one of these practices could be placed in the religion box if religion is viewed from the vantage point of meaning making.

If we examine the Pew surveys of religious life in the United States with meaning making as our guide, we might conclude that regular attendance at religious services is declining and fewer Americans are calling themselves Christian not because they are becoming *less* religious but because they are becoming *differently* religious. Americans are making meaning in more and different ways than belief in God, prayer, attendance at religious services, and self-identifying as Christian. We are not becoming more secular (whatever that might mean); we are

---

19. Smith, "Map Is Not Territory," 290–91.

merely becoming less distinctively Christian. In his landmark book *A Secular Age*, philosopher Charles Taylor refers to this phenomenon as a "break-down of previous religious forms," a "falling off, or alienation, from the Church."[20] In spite of this trend, says Taylor, human beings will continue to be religious. "I don't accept the view," he writes, "that the human aspiration to religion will flag."[21] It is merely changing.

CHANGE AND CHURCH

A 2007 survey by the Barna Group may help explain the change that Taylor describes. The Barna study found that Christianity has a "declining reputation" among Americans under thirty years old: "The study explored twenty specific images related to Christianity, including ten favorable and ten unfavorable perceptions. Among young non-Christians, nine out of the top 12 perceptions were negative. Common negative perceptions include that present-day Christianity is judgmental (87%), hypocritical (85%), old-fashioned (78%), and too involved in politics (75%). . . . Even among young Christians, many of the negative images generated significant traction. Half of young churchgoers said they perceive Christianity to be judgmental, hypocritical, and too political. One-third said it was old-fashioned and out of touch with reality."[22] One common expression among

---

20. Charles Taylor, *A Secular Age* (Cambridge, MA: Harvard University Press, 2018), 506, 520.

21. Taylor, 515.

22. "A New Generation Expresses Its Skepticism and Frustration with Christianity," Barna Group, September 21, 2007, https://tinyurl.com/vvgwve3.

those surveyed was that "Christianity in today's society no longer looks like Jesus."[23]

This negative perception of Christianity has been exacerbated recently by the overwhelming support for Donald Trump among evangelical Christians. Eighty-one percent of white evangelicals voted for Trump in 2016. This statistic led worship leader Daniel Deitrich to write a song titled "Hymn to the 81%," which expresses his grief and dismay. Deitrich accuses evangelicals of denying the teachings of Jesus and of turning religion into a bludgeon to pummel others. He is also horrified that evangelical support for Trump has been unwavering even after reports surfaced that migrant children along the southern US border were being taken from their mothers and confined in cages as part of the administration's zero-tolerance immigration policy. Deitrich sings that he needs to leave evangelicalism and look for Jesus somewhere else.[24]

Writer Jonathan Merritt also left evangelicalism and is now an important voice in progressive Christianity. Commenting on responses to the 2020 coronavirus outbreak by leading conservative clergy and theologians in the United States, Merritt wrote, "If the coronavirus is a test of our collective character, some American Christians are flat-out flunking." Merritt quotes Reformed theologian John Piper's response to the virus: "God sometimes uses disease to bring particular judgments upon those who reject him and give themselves over to sin." He quotes evangelical pastor Robert Jeffress: "All natural disasters can ultimately be traced back to sin." He also quotes

---

23. "New Generation."

24. See Shane Claiborne, "When Worship Is Resistance: Hymn for the 81%," Red Letter Christians, January 22, 2020, https://tinyurl.com/y3ekymgo.

Ralph Drollinger, the Christian minister who led Bible studies for Trump's cabinet members: "Whenever an individual or corporate group of individuals violate the inviolate precepts of God's Word, he, she, they, or the institution will suffer the respective consequences." Connecting human suffering on the scale of COVID-19 to sin, says Merritt, is the "kind of stark self-righteous insensitivity [that] makes nonreligious people despise Christians."[25] Studies like those conducted by the Barna Group support Merritt's conclusion.

SITUATING SIN

Besides being appalling examples of theological callousness (would you really look a grieving person in the eyes and tell them their loved one died because God sent the virus to punish them?), these perspectives cited by Merritt that link tragedy with sin raise all sorts of problematic questions. Even if we were to grant that God can punish human sin by sending natural disasters—a perspective found here and there in the Bible— how do we know that the specific tragedy of COVID-19 is a manifestation of God's wrath? Who can know the mind of God? Just because some stories in the Bible connect tragedy with sin doesn't necessarily mean that every tragedy in human history has been sent by God. The Bible doesn't speak with a single voice on the topic.

The one biblical book that deals exclusively with the topic of suffering actually makes the point that Job was innocent

---

25. Jonathan Merritt, "Some of the Most Visible Christians in America Are Failing the Coronavirus Test: In Place of Love, They're Offering Stark Self-Righteous Judgment," *Atlantic*, April 24, 2020, https://tinyurl.com/yxwv965t.

when tragedy struck. It was Job's friends who argued that his sin caused his suffering. God said they were wrong (Job 42:7). Beyond the biblical problems of connecting specific sins with specific tragedies, and beyond the fact that this perspective creates a monstrous image of God, there is also the problem of defining the category of sin. Conservative Christians like those Merritt quotes often isolate "homosexuality" as inciting God's wrath. Megachurch pastor John Hagee infamously said in a 2006 interview with Terry Gross on NPR's *Fresh Air* that Hurricane Katrina was sent by God to prevent a pride parade in New Orleans:

> I believe that New Orleans had a level of sin that was offensive to God, and they are—were recipients of the judgment of God for that. The newspaper carried the story in our local area that was not carried nationally that there was to be a homosexual parade there on the Monday that . . . Katrina came. And the promise of that parade was that it was going to reach a level of sexuality never demonstrated before in any of the other gay pride parades. So I believe that the judgment of God is a very real thing. . . . And I believe that . . . Hurricane Katrina was, in fact, the judgment of God against the city of New Orleans.[26]

My family and I lived in Toronto for five years and attended its fabulous pride parade each June. The weather was warm and sunny every year. Maybe God only judges American pride parades and not Canadian ones? As writer Anne Lamott once

---

26. John Hagee, "Pastor John Hagee on Christian Zionism," interviewed by Terry Gross, *Fresh Air*, NPR, September 18, 2006, audio, 23:09, https://tinyurl.com/yy2af2x6.

said, "You can safely assume you've created God in your own image when it turns out that God hates all the same people you do."[27]

Defining *sin* in the way Hagee defines it says more about Hagee than it does about sin. Viewing any tragedy as a manifestation of God's wrath says more about those who hold such a view than it does about God. This is because the ways in which we define categories—*sin, sacred, profane, God, secularization, believer, heretic, religion,* and so on—say more about us and our assumptions than they do about the people or things we are trying to classify. If God judges human sin with hurricanes and viruses, why is authentically living one's sexual orientation singled out as the particular object of God's wrath in the United States? What about gun violence, climate change, economic inequality, racism, white nationalism, injustice, mass incarceration, spending nearly a trillion dollars each year on defense while children go hungry, locking migrant human beings in cages, and the fact that millions of Americans lack affordable health care? When the Hebrew prophet Ezekiel rails against his fellow Israelites and likens them to the ancient city of Sodom, he points to their "pride, excess of food, and prosperous ease" that made them ignore "the poor and needy" (Ezek 16:49). If there's anything that incites God's wrath, says Ezekiel, it's injustice.

Those who single out the category of "homosexuality" as the special object of God's wrath often point to one New Testament passage in particular that they think justifies this view. When the apostle Paul writes about the "wrath of God [that] is revealed from heaven against all ungodliness and wickedness"

---

27. Anne Lamott, *Bird by Bird: Some Instructions on Writing and Life* (New York: Pantheon, 1994), 22.

(Rom 1:18), he mentions those who, in his words, "exchanged natural intercourse for unnatural" (Rom 1:26–27). In its context, this passage is Paul's way of talking about the things that he thinks are category mistakes, such as "exchang[ing] the glory of the immortal God for images resembling a mortal human being or birds or four-footed animals or reptiles" (Rom 1:23). Paul the monotheist sees idolatry as a quintessential confusion of categories: finite images of creation honored as if they were the infinite God. Paul also assumes that certain sexual practices fit into either natural or unnatural categories, and he places both idolatry and these sexual practices alongside a series of other actions that he says are unnatural: "Wickedness, evil, covetousness, malice . . . , envy, strife, etc." (Rom 1:29–32).

This series is what scholars call a vice list.[28] Lists of virtues and vices were common in antiquity—appearing in ancient Near East literature, Greco-Roman literature, the Old Testament, the writings of early Judaism, inscriptions of regulations that governed household religions, and the New Testament and other early Christian writings—and could serve a variety of purposes: educational, political, theological, and social. One social purpose that some of them served was to distinguish between the sacred and the profane.

An interesting example of this can be found in a Greek inscription from around 100 BCE that was created by a household religious group in the city of Philadelphia. The group chiseled into marble their origin story and a list of vices that they were to avoid. The marble inscription speaks of a man named Dionysios who was visited in a dream by the Greek god Zeus and given a series of regulations to govern the religious

---

28. See E. P. Sanders, *Paul: The Apostle's Life, Letters, and Thought* (Minneapolis: Fortress, 2015), ch. 12.

group that met in his house. The group was to avoid things like deception, harmful drugs, harmful spells, love potions, and adultery. Those who broke the rules, especially the rule against adultery, were, according to the inscription, "full of endemic pollution" because they were not abiding by the "sacred things" that Zeus told them to do. These naughty people exposed themselves to the wrath of the gods who would "inflict upon them great punishments."[29]

What makes the Philadelphia inscription so interesting to me is how similar it is to Paul's moral and theological language in Romans. The inscription distinguishes between sacred things and profane things in order to regulate people's behavior and thus define the boundaries of the group. Abide by the rules and you would remain a sacred insider; break them and the gods would treat you as a profane outsider. The rules themselves, according to the inscription, have a divine origin—they come from Zeus. Paul uses similar language in Romans. He classifies certain human behaviors as either natural or unnatural, and he traces the origin of this classification back to God. All unnatural behavior, says Paul, derives from what he believes is the fundamental category mistake of idolatry—a category mistake made by profane outsiders.

Paul's language and the language of the inscription both participate in what philosopher Michel Foucault called the same discursive field of ancient moral discourse. Although the specific details in their vice lists are different, the moral and theological structure of both lists is identical: both classify human behavior in sacred or profane categories, both trace the origin of this classification back to a divine source, and both

---

29. See Ascough, Harland, and Kloppenborg, *Associations in the Greco-Roman World*, 82–84.

threaten divine punishment for misbehavior. Like many others in the ancient world, both simply take this structure for granted because they assumed that the rules governing human behavior originated with the gods (or God), and they assumed that the gods (or God) who governed ancient groups and societies ultimately ensured that the rules were followed.

This structure can of course be found in various cultures in history, but it is problematic to uncritically yank Paul's moral and theological language out of its ancient context and apply it to the hurricanes and viruses of today. It is just as silly as trying to apply the rules of the Philadelphia inscription about harmful spells and love potions to us today. These are ancient documents that originated in a particular context when certain ideas were taken for granted. The categories of natural and unnatural, sacred and profane that appear in Paul's letter and in the inscription tell us about the ancient context, values, and assumptions of the creators of those categories and *not* whether those categories are still relevant today. So when some of today's clergy and theologians co-opt an ancient framework to declaim against certain "sins," and when they presume to know that God is punishing certain "sins" by sending hurricanes or viruses, they are making a choice to use Paul's language in this way. The categories they choose to use and the behaviors they choose to condemn tell us more about *them* and what *they* value or despise than they do about either God or sin.

This doesn't mean that we should dismiss as irrelevant every vice in New Testament vice lists or every theological statement in the Bible just because they are ancient. Placing the Bible in its ancient context reinforces for us as progressive Christians that the Bible is a place to start building a moral and theological framework. The Bible and the Christian tradition that has housed its interpretation provide a foundation that we build on, develop, renovate, and redesign. If, for example, we treated Paul's words in Romans as a place to start, we might choose to emphasize his idea that all the twisted behaviors of human beings originate with a category mistake. We could then ask, What category mistakes do we see today? Treating the planet as something to be dominated and subdued regardless of the effects on the climate might be one. The planet is our home. Why would we destroy our home and the home of billions of other living things? Asserting that the personal freedom to own an assault rifle is more important than keeping schoolchildren safe might be another way to build on Paul's ideas. Schools are supposed to be havens of learning, not war zones of death. Treating people as objects to exploit, lock in cages, or hate instead of as human beings created in God's image might be yet another way to develop Paul's ideas. People should be treated with compassion and love. They are sacred. No human being is profane.

A PROGRESSIVE CHURCH

What if we imagined church as a place where *no one is out*, where no one is *profane*? If the categories we create and the words we use to define those categories reveal our values and assumptions, then I will gladly plant my rainbow flag on the church lawn and declare that every person is sacred. I will gladly be like Louise in the story told by Tom Troeger and view every person as an insider. There are no outsiders. Isn't this how Jesus treated the Samaritan woman at the well, Zacchaeus the tax collector, the prostitute who washed his feet with her tears, the fumbling disciples, and the sundry sinners who flocked around him? Richard Rohr has said that "the only thing [Jesus] excluded was exclusion itself."[30]

The categories we create and the words we use to define those categories have effects. If we say that no one is out because every person is sacred, it changes how we see people, it changes how people see themselves, and it changes how we do church. In his book *To Take Place*, Jonathan Z. Smith examines religious rituals in places like ancient temples. "Within the temple," he writes, "the ordinary . . . becomes significant, becomes 'sacred,' simply by being there. . . . Something or someone is made sacred by ritual."[31] According to Smith, nothing is inherently sacred or profane; something is *made* sacred or profane by how it is treated. A table is just a table; it becomes sacred when the Communion bread and cup are placed on it and the words of institution are spoken. A church building is just wood and brick; it becomes a sacred space when we fill it with hymns and prayers. Prostitutes, tax collectors, Samaritan women, and fumbling disciples are not profane; they are made profane by how they are treated, but they become sacred when they are treated as sacred children of God. Isn't this how Jesus treated people in the gospels? And when Jesus rebuked people in the gospels (e.g., Matt 23), I imagine him doing so because he loved them too much to leave them unchanged and unchallenged; he was trying to love them into his own image—the incarnation of divine love.

My church in Ithaca is like many progressive churches across the country in that we strive to be a place where *no*

---

30. Rohr, *Universal Christ*, 34 (italics removed).

31. Jonathan Z. Smith, *To Take Place: Toward a Theory in Ritual* (Chicago: University of Chicago Press, 1987), 104–5.

one is out. The rainbow flag on our front lawn is a colorful way to proclaim this message to the entire Ithaca community. We also proclaim this message every Sunday when we greet people with the phrase "No matter who you are or where you are on life's journey, you are welcome here." We add to this phrase some special words of welcome for people who don't easily fit into the categories of gender, race, sexual orientation, socioeconomic status, belief, or age. We welcome those who are gender fluid, those who are in transition, those who are neither (or both) queer nor straight, those who are advanced in age but still young at heart, those who self-identify as biracial or multiracial, those who are spiritually and economically rich or poor, and those who occupy the penumbra around Christian doctrine—those who question, doubt, or take comfort in mystery.

Instead of focusing on belief, we talk about belonging. Believing a bunch of doctrines gleaned from ancient Christian creeds is not a requirement for belonging to our church; we say instead that everyone belongs whether they are believers, doubters, or a little bit of both. I underscore this message when I teach confirmation class. Confirmation in my tradition is the moment when teenagers decide for themselves to "affirm their baptism," a way of saying, "Although I was baptized as an infant, I am now taking ownership of my faith journey." Teenagers in my class are not required to believe certain things in order to be confirmed—they don't have to believe in order to belong. They only need to claim ownership over their own faith journey and know that the spiritual resources of the church stand ready to assist and support them for the rest of their lives. In class, we study the Bible, Christian tradition, current events, and J. K. Rowling's book *Harry Potter and the Sorcerer's Stone*. Harry belonged to the wizarding world long before he believed himself to be a wizard, and the same is true in church: we belong before or even whether we believe; we are sacred and beloved children of God whether or not we believe it. "You are a child of God, and always will be," writes Richard Rohr, "even when you don't believe it."[32] Before I teach a single lesson in confirmation class, I emphasize that the teenagers in the class already belong because I believe that God's spirit is more than capable of moving through them over the course of their lives to help them figure out the belief part.

To be a church where *no one is out* is to be a church of open doors, and I mean this literally. My church has opened its doors to other faith communities in town. A local Jewish community celebrates their High Holy Days in our sanctuary in the fall, and a local Muslim community has used our chapel five times a day for prayer. We are also a Sanctuary Church, which means that we have committed to housing an undocumented human being who is at risk of being deported. A room in our building has been converted to an apartment, and we are prepared to welcome children of God in need of a safe home as they try to gain legal status in our country.

But our congregation in upstate New York is not the only one engaged in these activities. Progressive Christian churches across the country are doing these things and more.[33] Some churches have become neighborhood hubs for community groups to gather. Others make space in their sanctuaries for local artists to display their work. I once visited a church in Los Angeles that recruited bands and musicians from bars in their neighborhood to lead worship on Sundays. Listening to a local

---

32. Rohr, *Universal Christ*, 37 (italics removed).

33. See examples in Jack Jenkins, *American Prophets: The Religious Roots of Progressive Politics and the Ongoing Fight for the Soul of the Country* (New York: HarperCollins, 2020); and Guthrie Graves-Fitzsimmons, *Just Faith: Reclaiming Progressive Christianity* (Minneapolis: Broadleaf, 2020).

band sing about love was one of the most powerful experiences I have ever had in church.

To be a place where *no one is out* blurs the lines between sacred and secular. It means that we are developing, renovating, and redesigning our ancient tradition to ensure that every person feels like they belong. It means that *Harry Potter and the Sorcerer's Stone* can be a confirmation class textbook. It means that Sunday worship could include the Beatles, Bob Dylan, Drake, Erik Satie, or Trent Reznor (we have played Reznor's somber song "A Warm Place" during our Good Friday services because it so beautifully captures the mood) alongside traditional hymns, anthems, and baroque-era postludes. Most of all, it means that we are creatively living into the foundational commandment of our tradition—love your neighbor as yourself—one of two commandments that Jesus said were essential (Matt 22:37–40).

The love command requires creativity because it lacks specificity. To love a neighbor may include being kind, doing no harm, tending to physical needs, being empathetic in times of suffering, giving food or water to a hungry or thirsty enemy who is also a neighbor, working for justice and peace, and countless other large and small gestures. The love command is ambiguous, which I think makes some people nervous. They prefer to know exactly what they are supposed to do, and so they are drawn to the moral clarity of New Testament vices lists, which they think define right and wrong in black-and-white terms. Centuries-old vice lists don't translate well to our time, but the love command is timeless. "Command" may not even be the best way to describe it, since it's more an invitation than a law. In his book *The Orthodox Heretic*, Peter Rollins asks, "What if Jesus was not offering his followers an ethical system to follow, but rather was inviting them to enter into a life of love that transcends ethics, a life of liberty that dwells beyond religious laws?"[34] Rollins illustrates this with a story:

> One day, a small group of disciples who had embraced the way of Jesus early in his ministry heard him preaching by the side of a dusty road. As they crowded round they heard Jesus say, "the law requires that you carry a pack for one mile, but I say carry it freely for two." The disciples were deeply impressed by these words, for at the time a Roman soldier had the legal right to demand that a citizen carry his pack for a mile as a service to the Empire. This teaching not only allowed the disciples to turn this oppressive law into an opportunity to demonstrate kingdom [of God] values, but also presented them with an opportunity to suffer in some small way for their faith. As it was common for soldiers to evoke this law, the small band of believers soon developed a reputation for their actions. Roman soldiers would often hope that the citizens they asked to carry their packs would be among these disciples, and often a small bond of friendship would develop between a soldier and these followers of the Way [of Jesus]. After a year had passed this custom had become so established in the group that it became a defining characteristic of their shared life. The leaders would frequently refer to the teaching of Jesus and emphasize the need to carry a pack of the Roman soldier for two miles as a sign of one's faith and commitment to God. It so happened that Jesus heard about this community's work, and, on his way to Jerusalem, took time to visit them. The leaders eagerly

---

34. Peter Rollins, *The Orthodox Heretic and Other Impossible Tales* (Brewster, MA: Paraclete, 2015), 45–46.

gathered all the members of the group to hear what Jesus would say. Once everyone had gathered, Jesus addressed them: "Dear brothers and sisters, you are faithful and honest, but I have come to you with a second message, for you failed to understand the first. Your law says that you must carry a pack for two miles. My law says, 'carry it for three.'"[35]

The invitation to love is not a law or a duty. "Love pushes us beyond duty," Rollins says. "If the ethical question is, 'What must be done?' love adds, 'I will do more.'"[36] The invitation to love is an invitation to go beyond a list of rules embedded in an ancient vice list; indeed, the invitation to love may require us to disagree with the Bible's classification of certain behaviors as vices. Rules that may have been seen as loving in the past may be downright cruel and hateful in the present because peoples and cultures change over time. But the invitation to love in our tradition is seen as foundational and timeless because it is an extension of God's very essence. "God is love," says the New Testament author of First John (1 John 4:8b).

I once heard a preacher creatively connect this statement with Paul's definition of love in 1 Corinthians 13:4–8a: "Love is patient; love is kind; love is not envious or boastful or arrogant or rude. It does not insist on its own way; it is not irritable or resentful; it does not rejoice in wrongdoing, but rejoices in the truth. It bears all things, believes all things, hopes all things, endures all things. Love never ends." She encouraged us in her sermon to combine the two passages. If God is love and if love is defined by Paul, then Paul is also telling us about who God is. She suggested that we replace the words *love* and *it* in

---

35. Rollins, 43–44.
36. Rollins, 47.

1 Corinthians 13 with the word *God*: "God is patient; God is kind; God is not envious or boastful or arrogant or rude. God does not insist on God's own way; God is not irritable or resentful; God does not rejoice in wrongdoing, but rejoices in the truth. God bears all things, believes all things, hopes all things, endures all things. God never ends." Her sermon was a beautiful example of creatively linking ethics with theology, providing a road map for how to live into love today.

At its core, progressive Christianity is an invitation to love. It's an invitation with deep, millennia-old ethical and theological roots that emanate outward in concentric circles from the triune circle of divine love. It's a divine love that envelops us and then challenges us to loosen our grip like Louise and let everyone in. This divine love troubles our categories, disrupts our systems of classifying people, erases the boundaries we establish between us and them, and frees us up to live more compassionately. Isn't this a more liberating and fulfilling way to live one's life of faith?

CONCLUSION: LOVE AND PROGRESSIVE CHRISTIANITY

If I have learned anything in my long life, it is that everything— everything: God, the Creation, the myriad creatures and processes of life, indeed life as such, and we humans who have been given the wherewithal to contemplate it all—everything is steeped in ineffable mystery. And if I were asked to say, in a word, what Christianity has contributed to this awareness of mystery, which has been felt by all great philosophies and religions and sciences, I would answer that Christianity professes and confesses that at the center of this universal

> *mystery there is … love. Eternal, forgiving, expectant, suffering love. That is why the life, death, and resurrection of Jesus, called the Christ, is the central image and narrative of the Christian faith: because his story announces so poignantly and unforgettably how love, despite all that negates and demeans it, is the origin and end of all that is: the* alpha *and* omega, *as the Scriptures say.*
>
> —Douglas John Hall, *What Christianity Is Not*

Saint Paul's vision in Philippians 2 of every knee bowing and every tongue confessing that Jesus is Lord is a vision of love—indeed, Christ is the incarnation of Love. Paul's vision is a vision of knees bowing before love and confessing with Douglas John Hall that love is "the origin and end of all that is: the *alpha* and *omega*."[37] It's an inspiring vision of hope. In the M. Night Shyamalan film *The Village*, Edward Walker, the village's chief elder, speaks of the power of love. "The world moves for love," he says. "It kneels before it in awe."[38] Walker's words echo Saint Paul's.

To say that love is at the core of progressive Christian identity is to make both a theological and an ethical claim. Theological: the triune God *is* love, existing in an eternal dance of communal love, becoming incarnate in the Christ, and flowing through the world by the power of the Spirit of Love. Ethical: our responsibility is to channel this Spirit of Love by living in love, connecting with Love through prayer, and thus conforming increasingly to the image of Christ, who is the image of Love (Rom 8:29). As we connect more deeply to this Spirit, allowing

---

37. Douglas John Hall, *What Christianity Is Not: An Exercise in "Negative" Theology* (Eugene, OR: Cascade, 2013).

38. M. Night Shyamalan, dir., *The Village* (Burbank, CA: Touchstone Pictures, 2004), DVD.

it to move through us, we can live more intentionally into the promise articulated by novelist Salman Rushdie that "love is stronger than hate."[39] We can live into the promises of the Hebrew prophets about swords being beaten into plowshares and wolves and lambs lying down in peace. We can be firmly anchored to what theologian Paul Tillich called "the ground of being," which is Love.[40] We can follow the example of Love incarnate—Christ. We can strive to interpret the Bible in loving ways that uplift instead of degrade human personality. And we can be free to risk throwing open our church doors to any and all in the strong confidence that Love, as Saint Paul once said, "never fails" (1 Cor 13:8a NIV) because Love is relentless, constantly striving to make sacred even the most desecrated people and things.

Love has the power to transform. At the compassionate core of progressive Christianity is a commitment to see every person as Christ sees them—as a beloved human being worthy of love and acceptance. In Luke's Gospel (17:11–19) ten lepers approach Jesus and cry out, "Jesus, Master, have mercy on us!" It's tempting for modern readers of the story to focus on the healing of the ten and on the effusive gratitude of the one who returned to Jesus to thank him. But the power of this story lies in the miracle of *seeing*. Even though the ten lepers were crying out to Jesus, Luke doesn't say that Jesus heard them—Luke says that Jesus "saw" them. After Jesus told them to show themselves to the priests to be pronounced clean, one of the lepers (a "Samaritan") "*saw* that he was healed" (italics mine). The miracle of the

---

39. Salman Rushdie, *Two Years, Eight Months, and Twenty-Eight Nights: A Novel* (New York: Random House, 2015), 234.

40. See Paul Tillich, *Systematic Theology*, vol. 1 (Chicago: University of Chicago Press, 1973).

story is a miracle of *seeing*: the leper *saw* himself as Jesus always *saw* him—beloved, pure, clean, beautiful, accepted. As progressive Christians, we strive to follow the example of Christ—the incarnation of Love—and see all of our fellow human beings as Christ sees them. And when we do, we can believe with hymn writer Rory Cooney that *the world is about to turn*.

RECOMMENDED RESOURCES

Arnal, William. *The Symbolic Jesus: Historical Scholarship, Judaism and the Construction of Contemporary Identity*. Religion in Culture. London: Equinox, 2005.

Bell, Rob. *What We Talk about When We Talk about God*. New York: HarperOne, 2013.

Bettenson, Henry, and Chris Maunder, eds. *Documents of the Christian Church*. New York: Oxford University Press, 1943. Reprint, New York: Oxford University Press, 2011.

Bolz-Weber, Nadia. *Accidental Saints: Finding God in All the Wrong People*. New York: Convergent Books, 2015.

Borg, Marcus J. *The Heart of Christianity: Rediscovering a Life of Faith*. San Francisco: HarperSanFrancisco, 2003.

———. *Meeting Jesus Again for the First Time: The Historical Jesus and the Heart of Contemporary Faith*. San Francisco: HarperSanFrancisco, 1994.

Butler Bass, Diana. *Christianity after Religion: The End of Church and the Birth of a New Spiritual Awakening*. New York: HarperOne, 2012.

Crossan, John Dominic. *How to Read the Bible and Still Be a Christian*. New York: HarperOne, 2015.

Gager, John G. *Reinventing Paul*. New York: Oxford University Press, 2000.

Hall, Douglas John. *Why Christian? For Those on the Edges of Faith*. Minneapolis: Fortress, 1998.

Keller, Catherine. *On the Mystery: Discerning Divinity in Process*. Minneapolis: Fortress, 2008.

McLaren, Brian D. *The Great Spiritual Migration: How the World's Largest Religion Is Seeking a Better Way to Be Christian*. New York: Convergent Books, 2016.

Nongbri, Brent. *Before Religion: A History of a Modern Concept.* New Haven, CT: Yale University Press, 2013.

Rohr, Richard. *The Universal Christ: How a Forgotten Reality Can Change Everything We See, Hope for, and Believe.* London: SPCK, 2019.

Rollins, Peter. *How (Not) to Speak of God.* Brewster, MA: Paraclete, 2006. Reprint, Brewster, MA: Paraclete, 2017.

Schüssler Fiorenza, Elisabeth. *In Memory of Her: A Feminist Theological Reconstruction of Christian Origins.* New York: Crossroad, 1983. Reprint, New York: Crossroad, 2005.

Smith, Jonathan Z. "Fences and Neighbors." In *Imagining Religion: From Babylon to Jonestown,* 1–18. Chicago: University of Chicago Press, 1982.

Spong, John Shelby. *A New Christianity for a New World: Why Traditional Faith Is Dying and How a New Faith Is Being Born.* San Francisco: HarperSanFrancisco, 2001.

Stellman, Jason. *Misfit Faith: Confessions of a Drunk Ex-paster.* New York: Convergent Books, 2017.

Tutu, Desmond. *God Has a Dream: A Vision of Hope for Our Time.* New York: Random House, 2004.

Wiman, Christian. *My Bright Abyss: Meditation of a Modern Believer.* New York: Farrar, Straus & Giroux, 2013.

BIBLIOGRAPHY

Alter, Robert. *The Book of Psalms: A Translation with Commentary.* New York: W. W. Norton, 2007.

Armstrong, Karen. "Let's Revive the Golden Rule." Filmed July 2009 in Oxford, UK. TED video, 9:54. https://tinyurl.com/y5mlk6us.

Arnal, William. *The Symbolic Jesus: Historical Scholarship, Judaism and the Construction of Contemporary Identity.* Religion in Culture. London: Equinox, 2005.

Ascough, Richard S., Philip A. Harland, and John S. Kloppenborg, eds. *Associations in the Greco-Roman World: A Sourcebook.* Waco, TX: Baylor University Press, 2012.

Ashcroft, Bill, Gareth Griffiths, and Helen Tiffin. *Post-colonial Studies: Key Concepts.* London: Routledge, 2000.

Aslan, Reza. *God: A Human History.* New York: Random House, 2017.

———. *Zealot: The Life and Times of Jesus of Nazareth.* New York: Random House, 2013.

Bentley Hart, David. *That All Shall Be Saved: Heaven, Hell, and Universal Salvation.* New Haven, CT: Yale University Press, 2019.

Bettenson, Henry, and Chris Maunder, eds. *Documents of the Christian Church.* New York: Oxford University Press, 1943. Reprint, New York: Oxford University Press, 2011.

Boorstein, Michelle. "Alabama State Official Defends Roy Moore, Citing Joseph and Mary: 'They Became Parents of Jesus.'" *Washington Post,* November 19, 2017. https://tinyurl.com/y6nhzbvq.

Borg, Marcus J. *The Heart of Christianity: Rediscovering a Life of Faith.* San Francisco: HarperSanFrancisco, 2003.

Boyle, Gregory. *Tattoos on the Heart: The Power of Boundless Compassion*. New York: Free Press, 2010.

Brown, Tim. *Change by Design: How Design Thinking Transforms Organizations and Inspires Innovation*. New York: Harper Business, 2009.

Brown, William. "Moabite Stone [Mesha Stele]." Ancient History Encyclopedia. February 11, 2019. https://tinyurl.com/y2895jgl.

Butler Bass, Diana. *Christianity after Religion: The End of Church and the Birth of a New Spiritual Awakening*. New York: HarperOne, 2012.

Calvin, John. *Institutes of the Christian Religion*. Edited by John T. McNeill. Translated by Ford Lewis Battles. Library of Christian Classics 20. 2 vols. Louisville, KY: Westminster John Knox, 1960.

"The Charter for Compassion." Charter for Compassion. Accessed February 26, 2021. https://charterforcompassion.org/charter/affirm.

Chesterton, G. K. *Orthodoxy*. New York: Snowball Classics, 2015.

Claiborne, Shane. "When Worship Is Resistance: Hymn for the 81%." Red Letter Christians, January 22, 2020. https://tinyurl.com/y3ekymgo.

Coogan, Michael. *The Old Testament: A Very Short Introduction*. New York: Oxford University Press, 2008.

Crossley, James G. "Halakah and Mark 7:3: 'With the Hand in the Shape of a Fist.'" *New Testament Studies* 58, no. 1 (2012): 57–68.

Douglas, Mary. *Purity and Danger: An Analysis of Concept of Pollution and Taboo*. London: Routledge & Kegan Paul, 1966. Reprint, New York: Routledge, 2002.

Douthat, Ross. "Save the Mainline." *New York Times*, April 15, 2017. https://tinyurl.com/y6ouqsd5.

Durkheim, Émile. *The Elementary Forms of Religious Life*. Translated by Karen E. Fields. New York: Free Press, 1995.

Eagleton, Terry. *Culture and the Death of God*. New Haven, CT: Yale University Press, 2014.

Eisenbaum, Pamela. "Jewish Perspectives: A Jewish *Apostle to the Gentiles*." In *Studying Paul's Letters: Contemporary Perspectives and Methods*, edited by Joseph A. Marchal, 135–153. Minneapolis: Fortress, 2012.

Eliade, Mircea. *The Sacred and the Profane: The Nature of Religion*. Translated by William R. Trask. London: Harcourt, 1987.

"English Cathedral Welcomes Visitors with Unexpected Message." *Weekend Edition Sunday*, NPR, January 15, 2017. https://tinyurl.com/y5ntxd9l.

"Faith and Doubt at Ground Zero." *Frontline*, PBS, September 3, 2002. https://tinyurl.com/y4w4knkt.

Foucault, Michel. *This Is Not a Pipe*. Edited and translated by James Harkness. Berkeley: University of California Press, 1983. Reprint, Berkeley: University of California Press, 2008.

Gager, John G. *Reinventing Paul*. New York: Oxford University Press, 2000.

Gallagher, Edmon L., and John D. Meade. *The Biblical Canon Lists from Early Christianity: Texts and Analysis*. New York: Oxford University Press, 2017.

Gaston, Lloyd. *Paul and the Torah*. Eugene, OR: Wipf & Stock, 1987.

George, Robert P., and Cornell West. "Sign the Statement: Truth Seeking, Democracy, and Freedom of Thought and Expression—a Statement by Robert P. George and Cornell West." James Madison Program in American Ideals and Institutions, March 14, 2017. http://jmp .princeton.edu/statement.

Graves-Fitzsimmons, Guthrie. *Just Faith: Reclaiming Progressive Christianity*. Minneapolis: Broadleaf, 2020.

Hagee, John. "Pastor John Hagee on Christian Zionism." Interviewed by Terry Gross. *Fresh Air*, NPR, September 18, 2006. Audio, 23:09. https://tinyurl.com/yy2af2x6.

Hall, Douglas John. *The Cross in Our Context: Jesus and the Suffering World*. Minneapolis: Fortress, 2003.

———. *What Christianity Is Not: An Exercise in "Negative" Theology*. Eugene, OR: Cascade, 2013.

Hitchens, Christopher. *Hitch-22: A Memoir*. New York: Twelve, 2010.

Holson, Laura M. "How Battles over Same-Sex Couples Play Out in Court." *New York Times*, July 17, 2019. https://tinyurl.com/y3yo4wav.

"In U.S., Decline of Christianity Continues at a Rapid Pace: An Update on America's Changing Religious Landscape." Pew Research Center, Washington, DC, October 17, 2019. https://tinyurl.com/y54m8cjv.

"In U.S., Smaller Share of Adults Identify as Christians, While Religious 'Nones' Have Grown." Pew Research Center, Washington, DC, October 16, 2019. https://tinyurl.com/y2eh2l2a.

Jacobs, Julia. "Sessions's Use of Bible Passage to Defend Immigration Policy Draws Fire." *New York Times*, June 15, 2018. https://tinyurl.com/ybx9r9qy.

Jenkins, Jack. *American Prophets: The Religious Roots of Progressive Politics and the Ongoing Fight for the Soul of the Country.* New York: HarperCollins, 2020.

Josephus. *Jewish War.* Translated by H. J. Thackeray. Vol. 3. Cambridge, MA: Harvard University Press, 2014.

Kaden, David A. "Flavius Josephus and the *Gentes Devictae* in Roman Imperial Discourse: Hybridity, Mimicry, and Irony in the Agrippa II Speech (*Judean War* 2.345–402)." *Journal for the Study of Judaism* 42, nos. 4–5 (2011): 481–507.

———. *Matthew, Paul, and the Anthropology of Law.* Wissenschaftliche Untersuchungen zum Neuen Testament no. 2. Tübingen: Mohr Siebeck, 2016.

Keller, Catherine. *Face of the Deep: A Theology of Becoming.* London: Routledge, 2003.

———. *On the Mystery: Discerning Divinity in Process.* Minneapolis: Fortress, 2008.

Keller, Catherine, and Laurel C. Schneider. Introduction to *Polydoxy: Theology of Multiplicity and Relation,* 1–15. London: Routledge, 2011.

King, Martin Luther, Jr. "Letter from Birmingham Jail." Stanford University, April 16, 1963. https://tinyurl.com/je2l2rg.

Lamott, Anne. *Bird by Bird: Some Instructions on Writing and Life.* New York: Pantheon, 1994.

Lewis, C. S. *A Grief Observed.* London: Faber, 1961. Reprint, New York: HarperCollins, 1989.

Lincoln, Bruce. *Holy Terrors: Thinking about Religion after September 11.* Chicago: University of Chicago Press, 2003. Reprint, Chicago: University of Chicago Press, 2006.

Marshall, John W. "Hybridity and Reading Romans." *Journal for the Study of the New Testament* 31, no. 2 (2008): 157–178.

Mazza, Ed. "Jim Bakker Says God Will Punish You for Making Fun of Him." *Huffington Post,* October 17, 2017. https://tinyurl.com/ycuqjdvc.

McCann, Colum. *Letters to a Young Writer.* New York: Random House, 2017.

McIntosh, Kenneth. *Water from an Ancient Well: Celtic Spirituality for Modern Life.* Vestal, NY: Anamchara Books, 2011.

McLaren, Brian D. *The Great Spiritual Migration: How the World's Largest Religion Is Seeking a Better Way to Be Christian.* New York: Convergent Books, 2016.

Mealer, Bryan. "How I Became Christian Again: My Long Journey to Find Faith Once More." *Guardian*, December 25, 2017. https://tinyurl.com/y8ov7qta.

Merritt, Jonathan. "The Rise of the Christian Left in America: The Religious Right Has Been in Decline for Years. Can Progressives Build a New 'Moral Majority?'" *Atlantic*, July 25, 2013. https://tinyurl.com/y8lmvuhu.

———. "Some of the Most Visible Christians in America Are Failing the Coronavirus Test: In Place of Love, They're Offering Stark Self-Righteous Judgment." *Atlantic*, April 24, 2020. https://tinyurl.com/yxwv965t.

Merton, Thomas. *Contemplative Prayer*. Louisville, KY: Merton Legacy Trust, 1969. Reprint, New York: Doubleday, 1996.

Miles, Jack. *God: A Biography*. New York: Vintage Books, 1995.

Moss, Candida. *The Myth of Persecution: How Early Christians Invented a Story of Martyrdom*. New York: HarperOne, 2013.

Nail, Thomas. *Theory of the Border*. New York: Oxford University Press, 2016.

Newell, J. Philip. *Listening for the Heartbeat of God: A Celtic Spirituality*. London: SPCK, 1997.

"A New Generation Expresses Its Skepticism and Frustration with Christianity." Barna Group, September 21, 2007. https://tinyurl.com/vvgwve3.

Nietzsche, Friedrich. *Beyond Good and Evil: Prelude to a Philosophy of the Future*. Translated by Helen Zimmern. Stilwell, KS: Digireads, 2005.

———. *Thus Spoke Zarathustra: A Book for All and None*. Translated by Thomas Common. North Charleston, SC: Pantianos Classics, 2016.

Nongbri, Brent. *Before Religion: A History of a Modern Concept*. New Haven, CT: Yale University Press, 2013.

Norris, Pippa, and Ronald Inglehart. *Sacred and Secular: Religion and Politics Worldwide*. Cambridge: Cambridge University Press, 2004. Reprint, Cambridge: Cambridge University Press, 2013.

Placher, William C. *Narratives of a Vulnerable God: Christ, Theology, and Scripture*. Louisville, KY: Westminster John Knox, 1994.

"Reimagining the Shopping Cart." Ideo. Accessed February 26, 2021. https://tinyurl.com/y6cramh6.

"Religious Landscape Study: Belief in God." Pew Research Center, June 4–September 30, 2014. http://www.pewforum.org/religious-landscape-study/.

Rohr, Richard. *Just This: Prompts and Practices for Contemplation.* London: SPCK, 2017.

———. *The Universal Christ: How a Forgotten Reality Can Change Everything We See, Hope for, and Believe.* London: SPCK, 2019.

Rollins, Peter. *How (Not) to Speak of God.* Brewster, MA: Paraclete, 2006. Reprint, Brewster, MA: Paraclete, 2017.

———. *Insurrection: To Believe Is Human, to Doubt, Divine.* New York: Howard Books, 2011.

———. *The Orthodox Heretic and Other Impossible Tales.* Brewster, MA: Paraclete, 2009. Reprint, Brewster, MA: Paraclete, 2015.

Rosaldo, Renato. *Ilongot Headhunting 1883–1974: A Study in Society and History.* Stanford, CA: Stanford University Press, 1980.

Ruether, Rosemary. *Faith and Fratricide: The Theological Roots of Anti-Semitism.* Eugene, OR: Wipf & Stock, 1995.

Rushdie, Salman. *Two Years, Eight Months, and Twenty-Eight Nights: A Novel.* New York: Random House, 2015.

Russell, William R., ed. *Martin Luther's Basic Theological Writings.* Minneapolis: Fortress, 2012.

Sagan, Carl. *The Varieties of Scientific Experience: A Personal View of the Search for God.* New York: Penguin, 2006.

Sanders, E. P. *Paul: The Apostle's Life, Letters, and Thought.* Minneapolis: Fortress, 2015.

———. *Paul and Palestinian Judaism: A Comparison of Patterns of Religion.* Minneapolis: Fortress, 1977.

Sansal, Boualem. *2084: The End of the World.* Translated by Alison Anderson. New York: Europa Editions, 2017.

Schmalz, Timothy P. "Homeless Jesus." Sculpture by Timothy P. Schmalz. Accessed February 26, 2021. https://tinyurl.com/y3pxzd9x.

Schultz, Daniel. "Jesus, Mary, Joseph: The Disgusting Religious Defense of Roy Moore." *Religion Dispatches*, November 10, 2017. https://tinyurl.com/y5vbsffr.

Schüssler Fiorenza, Elisabeth. *In Memory of Her: A Feminist Theological Reconstruction of Christian Origins.* New York: Crossroad, 1983. Reprint, New York: Crossroad, 2005.

———. *Jesus and the Politics of Interpretation*. New York: Continuum, 2001.

———. *Rhetoric and Ethic: The Politics of Biblical Studies*. Minneapolis: Fortress, 1999.

Sloterdijk, Peter. *God's Zeal: The Battle of the Three Monotheisms*. Translated by Wieland Hoban. Cambridge: Polity, 2009.

———. *In the Shadow of Mount Sinai: A Footnote on the Origins and Changing Forms of Total Membership*. Translated by Wieland Holan. Cambridge: Polity, 2016.

———. *Spheres*. Vol. 1, *Bubbles, Microspherology*. Translated by Wieland Hoban. South Pasadena, CA: Semiotext(e), 2011.

———. *Spheres*. Vol. 2, *Globes, Microspherology*. Translated by Wieland Hoban. South Pasadena, CA: Semiotext(e), 2014.

Smith, Jonathan Z. "Fences and Neighbors." In *Imagining Religion: From Babylon to Jonestown*, 1–18. Chicago: University of Chicago Press, 1982.

———. "Map Is Not Territory." In *Map Is Not Territory: Studies in the History of Religions*, 289–309. Chicago: University of Chicago Press, 1993.

———. "Sacred Persistence: Toward a Redescription of Canon." In *Imagining Religion: From Babylon to Jonestown*, 36–52. Chicago: University of Chicago Press, 1982.

———. *To Take Place: Toward a Theory in Ritual*. Chicago: University of Chicago Press, 1987.

Smith, Mark S. *The Early History of God: Yahweh and the Other Deities in Ancient Israel*. San Francisco: HarperSanFrancisco, 1990. Reprint, Grand Rapids, MI: Eerdmans, 2002.

Spong, John Shelby. *A New Christianity for a New World: Why Traditional Faith Is Dying and How a New Faith Is Being Born*. San Francisco: HarperSanFrancisco, 2001.

Stanger, Allison. "Understanding the Angry Mob at Middlebury That Gave Me a Concussion." *New York Times*, March 13, 2017. https://tinyurl.com/yyp3rw84.

Stanley, Christopher D., ed. *The Colonized Apostle: Paul through Postcolonial Eyes*. Minneapolis: Fortress, 2011.

"Statement by Alabama Clergy." Stanford University, April 12, 1963. https://tinyurl.com/y7d54kks.

Stroman, John A. *Out of the Whirlwind: First Lesson Sermons for Sundays after Pentecost (Last Third), Cycle B*. Lima, OH: CSS, 1999.

Taylor, Charles. *A Secular Age*. Cambridge, MA: Harvard University Press, 2007. Reprint, Cambridge, MA: Harvard University Press, 2018.

Thiessen, Matthew. *Jesus and the Forces of Death: The Gospels' Portrayal of Ritual Impurity within First-Century Judaism*. Grand Rapids, MI: Baker, 2020.

Tillich, Paul. *Systematic Theology*. Vol. 1. Chicago: University of Chicago Press, 1973.

"Todd Starnes and Dr. Robert Jeffress." Fox News, September 23, 2019. https://tinyurl.com/y4ynktnw.

Tyrrell, George. *Christianity at the Crossroads*. London: Longman, Green, 1910.

"U.S. Public Becoming Less Religious: Modest Drop in Overall Rates of Belief and Practice, but Religiously Affiliated Americans Are as Observant as Before." Pew Research Center, Washington, DC, November 3, 2015. https://tinyurl.com/yyh3lu36.

Viola, Frank. "Bono on Jesus." Patheos, October 3, 2016. https://tinyurl.com/ohdf8zy.

Watson, Francis. *Gospel Writing: A Canonical Perspective*. Grand Rapids, MI: Eerdmans, 2013.

Westboro Baptist Church (website). Accessed February 26, 2021. http://www.godhatesfags.com/index.html.

Williams, Demetrius K. "African American Approaches: Rehumanizing the Reader against Racism and Reading through Experience." In *Studying Paul's Letters: Contemporary Perspectives and Methods*, edited by Joseph A. Marchal, 155–173. Minneapolis: Fortress, 2012.

Wiman, Christian. *My Bright Abyss: Meditation of a Modern Believer*. New York: Farrar, Straus & Giroux, 2013.

Winter, Bruce W. *Divine Honours for the Caesars: The First Christians' Responses*. Grand Rapids, MI: Eerdmans, 2015.

Wright, N. T. *Paul and the Faithfulness of God*. Books 1–4. Minneapolis: Fortress, 2013.

Zauzmer, Julie, and Keith McMillan. "Sessions Cites Bible Passage Used to Defend Slavery in Defense of Separating Immigrant Families." *Washington Post*, June 15, 2018. https://tinyurl.com/uxxj4cl.

Žižek, Slavoj. *The Puppet and the Dwarf: The Perverse Core of Christianity*. Cambridge, MA: MIT Press, 2003.